best hikes with dogs

NEW JERSEY

best hikes with dogs

NEW JERSEY

Mary Jasch

THE MOUNTAINEERS BOOKS

Dedicated to Cleo, Farley, Little One, Petey, Tank, and Arnuk

THE MOUNTAINEERS BOOKS
is the nonprofit publishing arm of The Mountaineers Club, an organization
founded in 1906 and dedicated to the exploration, preservation, and
enjoyment of outdoor and wilderness areas.

1001 SW Klickitat Way, Suite 201, Seattle, WA 98134

First edition, 2007

Manufactured in the United States of America

Copy Editor: Brenda Pittsley
Cover and Book Design: The Mountaineers Books
Layout: Peggy Egerdahl
Cartographer: Pease Press Cartography
All photos by author unless otherwise noted.

Cover photograph: *Petey*
Frontispiece: *Spring, Daisy and Sunshine ready to hike the Appalachian Trail*

Maps shown in this book were produced using National
Geographic's TOPO! software. For more information,
go to *www.nationalgeographic.com/topo*.

Library of Congress Cataloging-in-Publication Data
Jasch, Mary.
  Best hikes with dogs in New Jersey / by Mary Jasch.—1st ed.
    p. cm.
  ISBN 1-59485-003-8 (ppb)
  1. Hiking with dogs—New Jersey—Guidebooks. 2. Trails—New
Jersey—Guidebooks. 3. New Jersey—Guidebooks. I. Title.
SF427.455.J37 2007
796.5109749—dc22

                              2006030380

CONTENTS

The Highlands

The Central Piedmont

The Southern Coastal Plains

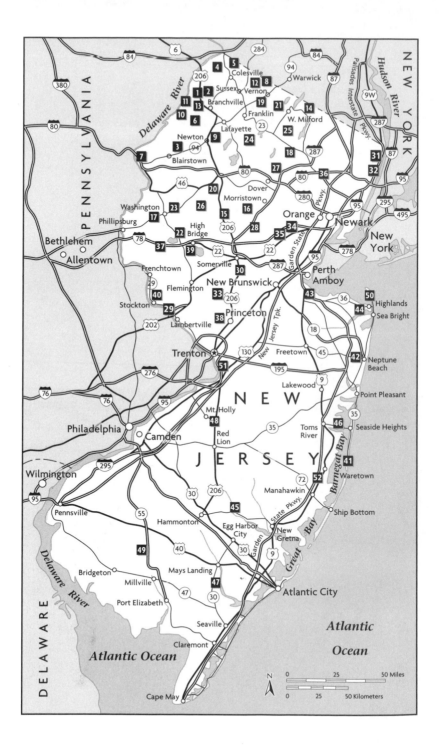

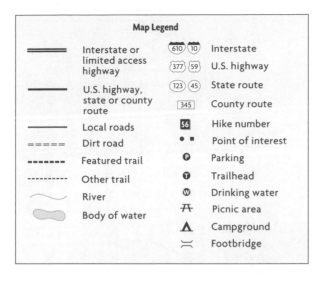

Map Legend

═══	Interstate or limited access highway	(610)(10) Interstate
────	U.S. highway, state or county route	(377)(59) U.S. highway
───	Local roads	(123)(45) State route
=====	Dirt road	[345] County route
-------	Featured trail	**56** Hike number
----------	Other trail	● ■ Point of interest
～	River	**P** Parking
⬮	Body of water	**T** Trailhead
		W Drinking water
		⊼ Picnic area
		▲ Campground
		≍ Footbridge

The way to route 94.

Trail	For Seniors	Experienced Dogs Only	Stream or Lake Along the Trail	Backpacking Opportunities	Loops	5 Miles and Over	Shorter Hike Possible	Best with Two Cars
The Northwest Ridge Valley								
1. Stepping-Stone Trail	●		●					
2. Sunrise Mountain Road Loop	● IS		●	●	●		●	
3. Paulinskill Valley Trail: Hainesburg to Blairstown	● SH		●		●	●	●	●
4. Cedar Swamp Trail	●		●	●	●			
5. Appalachian Trail: Wantage Foothills	● 1W		●	●		●	●	●
6. Spring Lake Loop	●		●		●			
7. Karamac–Dunnfield Creek Loop	● IS	●	●	●	●	●		
8. Pochuck Boardwalk	●		●	●	●			
9. Sussex Branch: Warbasse Junction to Augusta Hill Road	● 1W		●			●	●	●
10. Buttermilk Falls Loop		●	●			●	●	●
11. Tillman Ravine	●		●		●			
12. Appalachian Trail: Vernon Valley			●	●		●	●	●
13. Appalachian Trail: Culvers Lake to Buttermilk Falls		●	●	●		●	●	●
The Highlands								
14. Old Guard Trail		●	●			●	●	●
15. Hacklebarney Loop			●		●			
16. Jockey Hollow: Primrose Brook Loop	●		●		●			
17. Merrill Creek Reservoir: Perimeter Trail			●			●	●	●
18. Pyramid Mountain Loop		●	●		●			
19. Terrace Pond		●	●		●			
20. Schooley's Mountain: Boulder Gorge Loop			●		●			
21. Bearfort Ridge: Surprise Lake Loop		●	●	●	●	●		
22. Columbia Trail: High Bridge to Ken Lockwood Gorge	●		●			●	●	
23. Lake Marguerite–Griffith Woods Loop	●		●		●			
24. Mahlon Dickerson Reservation: Pine Swamp Loop			●		●	●		

Trail	For Seniors	Experienced Dogs Only	Stream or Lake Along the Trail	Backpacking Opportunities	Loops	5 Miles and Over	Shorter Hike Possible	Best with Two Cars
25. Norvin Green Vista Circuit		•	•		•	•	•	
26. Point Mountain Riverwalk Loop	•		•		•			
27. Tourne Park					•			
The Central Piedmont								
28. Lord Stirling Stable Dog Walk			•		•			
29. D&R Canal Towpath: Prallsville Mill and Lock to Lambertville	• IS		•			•	•	•
30. Six Mile Run Reservoir			•		•		•	
31. Palisades: Alpine Loop		•	•		•	•	•	
32. Palisades: Englewood Loop		•	•		•	•	•	
33. Sourland Mountain Ridge Trail			•		•		•	
34. Watchung Reservation: Green Brook Loop			•		•	•	•	
35. Watchung Reservation: Lake Surprise Loop	•		•		•		•	
36. Garret Mountain Loop	• IS		•		•		•	
37. Hoffman Park	•		•		•		•	
38. Mountain Lakes Nature Preserve	•		•		•		•	
39. Round Valley Loop	•		•		•	•		
40. Wickecheoke Creek Preserve	• IS		•				•	
The Southern Coastal Plains								
41. Island Beach	• IS		S				•	
42. Shark River Loop	•		•		•		•	
43. Cheesequake Blue Trail Loop	•		S		•			
44. Hartshorne Woods: Grand Tour Trail					•		•	
45. Batsto Village Loop	•		•		•			
46. Cattus Island	•		S		•			
47. Estell Manor Loop	• IS		•		•		•	
48. Historic Smithville Loop	•		•		•		•	
49. Parvin State Park Loop			•		•	•	•	
50. Sandy Hook: Beach and Dunes Loop			S		•	•	•	
51. Trenton-Hamilton Marsh	•		•		•		•	
52. Wells Mills Loop			•		•	•	•	

IS = in shape   SH = shorter hike   1W = one way   S = salt

ACKNOWLEDGMENTS

South Dune Trail, Sandy Hook

I want to thank all the people who helped me prepare this book, especially Lance L. Casper, for spending many weekends hiking with me in bear country, and my mother, Gertrude Mohn, and son, Paul, for their support. Thanks to all who shared the trails with me: Robert Boyle, Kathleen Casey, William Clother, Richard Flint, Sue Ellen Helmacy, Robert C. Jennings, Kerri Messinger, John Moran, Kristine Nelson, and Kathryn Ptacek.

Thanks to Doc Paul Tallamy for his advice and care of my four dogs and others in this book. And thanks to all the federal, state, county, township, and nature organization employees who took the time to make sure my information was accurate. Further thanks to Laura D. for her patience and humor, and to Margaret S., Kathleen C. and Maria C. for their courtesy and help in getting this book done.

A special round of applause goes to all the dogs who had a great time on the trails with me and my fellow hikers, and to dog owners everywhere who get out and hike with their pals. My special appreciation goes to Farley, Petey, Little One, and Tank—my big guys who all became great trail dogs, obedient while totally entranced by the sights, scents, and sounds of the trail.

AUTHOR'S NOTE

My first inkling of how great a dog can be as an outdoors companion came when, as a natural resources student at Cook College, Rutgers University, I researched plants and soils in New Jersey's tucked-away freshwater marshes. Arnuk, my son's German shepherd, kept me company. She was my eyes and ears in those secluded places. It was then I learned to read a dog reading the woods. And it was then that I realized how safe I felt alone in the woods with a dog. I was dogsitting Arnuk while my son, Paul, attended basic training in the United States Air Force.

Adventures with my own four canine pals began when, on August 18, 1995, Arnuk gave birth to eight pups. I kept four—three males and one female—Farley, Little One, Petey, and Tank. When they were three months old, the man in my life died. This instant canine support group helped me through that tough time. They are my best buddies, well-behaved trail dogs all. But it didn't come easy.

I lived in a quiet neighborhood with a fenced-in suburban yard when they were born. I watched them constantly as they played outside, enthusiastically as eight big pups will. I was ready to quell the slightest fracas. Jerry called them "The Panzer Division." Four went to live with great families, but the dilemma remained—how to give my new pals the exercise they needed, all at the same time.

When they were one year old, I heard about sled dog driving and found a gentleman who had driven a sled dog team for the Coast Guard in Labrador during World War II. He also drove a dog team in 30-mile mid-distance races. He taught me how to train my dogs to pull a three-wheeled gig (not much snow in New Jersey) and to teach them to sit quietly as I harnessed and hooked them to a gangline. They did well enough for recreation and exercise, but the gentleman aged and we began training with sprint dog teams. Misss-take! Instead of sitting quietly and behaving, they picked up the tension of the lunging northern-breed dogs who were always at the ready to run. My four pals became hyper and fought. After two years, we quit. The dogs and I were much happier then, but we still needed exercise.

I moved to the eroded old mountains of northwestern New Jersey and fell in love with the woods. Petey, my first trail dog, stayed always by my side, sniffing plants and flowers. He, my friend Kathleen, and I spent five days on our first backpack on the Appalachian Trail. Petey hiked with me everywhere, and every year we did another section of the AT. But in 2004, arthritis ended his long trail days—and he's glad to be off the trail.

Farley is my new trail buddy. He loves meeting new people and discovering the challenges of a long, difficult trail. Little One goes for short, easy walks, and Tank, never before calm on a leash, has made a successful maiden hike for this book. When the dogs see my pack and watch me gather gear or leash, they show me they're ready. They beg with their eyes to be chosen—except for Petey.

Coming home, my hike-of-the-day pal stretches across the back seat of the car. In the house, he stands tall for the others to sniff the scents of his day, then curls up in the big stuffed chair in the kitchen.

PART 1

Hiking Tips for Dogs and People

Let's hike! (Sunshine, Spring, and Daisy)

Life in the Slow Lane

Want to get away from it all? Grab your favorite canine buddy and a leash, and hop in your car. Head for the hills of northwest Jersey or the sandy flats of south Jersey. None are far from your own backyard. And what a thrill for Bowser—back to nature! At last!

Abundant opportunities to enjoy nature and escape a hectic world await people and their canine pals in New Jersey's national, state, county, and township parks and forests. Some private organizations also open their lands for people and dogs to experience.

Parks, forests, and other green space cover more than 1,066,000 acres or 22 percent of New Jersey's total land. With a population of 8,414,350 humans and an estimated 1.7 million dogs in the Garden State, everyone needs to have good trail manners.

The Misunderstood Dog, or Good Dogs Require Good Owners

Reasons abound for banning Bowser from scenic boardwalks and vistas. The basis for most of these reasons lies in fable or in faulty humans. Dogs are barred when people complain about them. What can be done? Don't give them cause for complaint! The power is in your hands.

Dogs scare wildlife. Let's face it, who scares a bird or a bear more—you or your dog? Dogs on leashes cannot chase and annoy wildlife. Keep your dog on a 6-foot maximum leash and teach him not to bark at animals.

Dogs annoy visitors. Birders travel long distances to come to New Jersey's flyways to see migrating birds, especially along the Atlantic Ocean, Kittatinny Ridge, and Delaware River. They do not want to risk a successful bird-watching trip because dogs scared birds away. Enough complaints may instigate a ban on four-legged beasts. Maintain control and teach dogs not to bark.

Dogs do their business right on the boardwalk. Whose fault is this? Know your dog and anticipate his needs. Take your dog off the boardwalk and pick up after him. Let everyone see how responsible you are as a representative of all dog owners.

Dogs scare people. Not everyone likes dogs. Keep your dog close to you when other people and dogs approach. Be courteous and you will leave people with a surprisingly good feeling that maybe "man's best friend" truly is.

Dogs scare other dogs. Be courteous and shorten your pet's leash to appease another dog owner's concern and move steadily onward. You will leave people who are apprehensive with a good and safe experience.

Canine Trail Etiquette

When people visit the woods or the beach, they might as well wear invisible "Do Not Disturb" signs. Create a fabulous impression by teaching Fido good manners, either personally or through a local obedience school. It is a joy to walk a well-behaved dog along a creek in solitude or on a popular towpath. Some good tips follow. Make your mark!

Aside from being outlawed in many New Jersey parks, a retractable leash allows a dog more line to explore farther away from the owner while being tethered. Many things can happen in this distance and in the time it takes to reel in the dog. He can chase small wildlife, get into a fight with a loose or unfriendly dog, jump up on people, and even snap at over-friendly kids and adults. Most parks also *require* that you have Fido under control at all times. It is almost impossible to control a dog who is 15 feet away and growling at another edgy dog. Keep your best pal out of trouble. Use a nylon web or leather leash no longer than 6 feet with a cushiony handle to keep your dog comfortably close.

One of Farley's favorite things about hiking is meeting new people. He shakes paws with Suely and Ray at Mountain Lakes Nature Preserve in Princeton.

Right-of-way. On most New Jersey trails, hikers yield to horses and bikers yield to hikers, but the rules can vary from one park to the next. Given the bad reputation dogs have in some places, it is important to put your dog's best paw forward. Be polite and step aside with your pooch, whether you have the right-of-way or not. Your good manners will not go unnoticed.

Other dogs. Not all dogs like other dogs. Some are antisocial. Some are afraid. When you approach another dog and hiker team, ask whether Fido is friendly, and keep your dog close to you. Dogfights are one of the primary reasons that dogs are not allowed in campsites.

On his best behavior. Is your dog a good boy on a leash? Can you control his primal urges? New Jersey, regrettably, is not Thoreauland, where an adventuresome cow—or canine—can break free and be beautiful. Instead, the leash law is everywhere. But with a well-behaved dog and courteous human, anything is possible—roads can be crossed, trails shared, and dogs and wildlife can live in hiking bliss. Let Fido be a doggy ambassador!

Basic Commands

To get the most fun and reward from his hike, your dog should be dog- and people-friendly and know basic commands for safety. Most can be taught at home. If your dog still has a few shortcomings, do him a favor and take him to an obedience class. Most communities have them, and he will probably enjoy the experience, especially if he needs to socialize. Then Fido's behavior on the trail is up to you. With your watchful eye, always be one step ahead of your dog in order to use these commands well. Use praise and positive reinforcement in anything you do with your dog in daily life.

Come! You are responsible for your dog's safety on the trail. Off-leash or unfriendly dogs, wild critters, and hikers who are interested in your tired pal are all potential problems, which you can prevent by teaching your dog to come. To teach your dog to come, gently reel him in like a fish and praise him when he comes to you. Overdo the praise with sensitive or apprehensive dogs to make obeying a positive experience. Read your dog's temperament.

Leave it! This is a great command to use when curious Bowser wants to stick his face in a hole where a snake or other trouble might wait, or when passing a carcass or other dog delight that may be unsafe. If your dog retrieves, don't let him; it could be a timber rattler instead of a stick. To teach him, give the dog a pop on the leash, command "Leave it!" and walk the other way. Practice at home until he learns that no matter what he sees, he should leave it and follow you wherever you go.

Quiet! Nobody likes barking dogs, especially on the trail. Life is hard enough. People will hate your dog and others just because you didn't teach him to be quiet. To teach him, say "Quiet!" in a firm tone. If he listens to you, say "Good quiet." Ignore any negative behavior. A basic obedience class can be an effective cure for unwelcome barking.

Wait! This is a good command that comes naturally to you and

Good dogs wait for orders. (Bob with Sunshine, Spring and Daisy)

your dog. It tells your dog to stop in his tracks for any reason you like. To teach him, say "Wait!" and stop. He will learn to stop with you.

Release command. From day one, teach him that the other end of "Sit, stay" is a release word so he understands when to move forward. This command helps ensure your dog's safety. For example, when you arrive in a parking lot and open the doors of your car, how will your dog know when it is safe to exit? If he has a release word, he knows he must remain in place until he hears the word. Choose an uncommon word that he won't hear often in normal conversation. I knew a dog whose release word was "SpaghettiOs."

Permits and Regulations

All of New Jersey's public lands are for you and your dog to enjoy every day. Hiking them is entertainment, therapy, and exercise for you both. So, get out and hike!

Delaware Water Gap National Recreation Area

More than 25 miles of the Appalachian National Scenic Trail (AT) lie within the Delaware Water Gap National Recreation Area (DWGNRA), which also has many other fun trails for day hikes of all lengths.

Hiking. Carry enough water for the entire hike, especially in summer. Water is scarce on Kittatinny Ridge, and found water must be chemically treated or boiled for five minutes. People and pets should stay on trails due to the sensitive nature of surrounding habitat. Carry out all trash. Hikers yield to horses, and bikers yield to hikers.

Camping. To camp overnight on the Appalachian Trail, hikers must be on the trail for at least two days, going from point A to point B. Camp within 100 feet of the AT, but not within 100 feet of any water source. Small backpack stoves are allowed, but not ground fires. Pitch your tent at least 200 feet from another tent. Camping is not permitted from 0.5 mile south of Blue Mountain Lake Road to 1 mile north of Crater Lake.

This is bear country, so store food in sealed containers—freezer bags work great. Hoist a sack containing food, cosmetics, and cooking utensils over a tree limb 10 feet high and 8 feet out from the trunk. Check your pockets and your dog's pack for any dog food, snacks, or wrappers, and be meticulous when eating and cleaning up. Pick up all scraps and keep the campsite clean.

Farley, waiting to hike!

Bury human and canine waste 6 inches deep and 100 feet from any trail, stream, road, or facility. Let Bowser carry a garden trowel and toilet paper in his pack.

Another option for camping outdoors is the dog-friendly Appalachian Mountain Club's Mohican Outdoor Center in Blairstown, with cabins, tent sites, showers, and cooking facilities. Call (908) 362-5670 or visit *www.mohicanoutdoorcenter.com*.

Dogs. Dogs must be on a leash no longer than 6 feet. Clean up after your dog. Dogs are not allowed at the Kittatinny Point Visitor Center and picnic area or the Watergate Recreation Site. If your dog gets lost (unlikely on a leash!), call park dispatch at (800) 543-4295. Service dogs are not regulated as pets.

Gateway National Recreation Area, Sandy Hook Unit

The 6.5-mile barrier beach peninsula offers 2044 acres of hiking trails along bay and ocean and through a maritime American holly forest.

Hiking. The park's carry-in/carry-out policy means take your trash home; leave nothing behind. Check at the visitor center when you arrive for updated information on beach closings or other restrictions. Open daily 10:00 AM to 5:00 PM. The beach area south of Gunnison Beach is posted as a clothing-optional area.

Dogs. Dogs must be on a leash no longer than 6 feet. Dogs are al-

lowed on ocean beaches from the day after Labor Day through March 14 only, to protect the endangered piping plover and other nesting shorebirds. Dogs are welcome on bayside beaches year-round. Stay on trails or beach, but keep off sensitive dunes. Clean up after your dog, and carry out waste.

Other information. There is a parking fee from Memorial Day through Labor Day. The Sandy Hook Lighthouse is the oldest lighthouse in the United States. It is open for tours on weekends from April through November. Call the visitor center at (732) 872-5970.

Rosy steeplebush (Spiraea tomentosa) *along the Paulinskill Valley Trail*

New Jersey Department of Environmental Protection, Division of Parks and Forestry

More than 300,000 acres comprise New Jersey's thirty-nine state parks and eleven state forests, with many trails passing through forty-three Natural Areas (parcels of land preserved in perpetuity due to their significant ecosystems as part of the state's Natural Areas System). Magnificent state parks and forests exist amid the densely populated areas of this small state. They are to be treasured.

Hiking. A trail for every hiker exists within state parks and forests in every part of New Jersey. From easy-to-hike flat abandoned railroad beds to the rugged Kittatinny Ridge in the Northwest Ridge and Valley; from gentle trails of estates-turned-parks to mountainous peaks in the Highlands; from flat canal towpaths to the volcanic Watchungs in the Central Piedmont; and from ocean beaches to lengthy sand roads in the Coastal Plain—there is a "no excuses" trail for everyone.

Camping. Dogs are not allowed to camp overnight in any state park or forest except along the Appalachian Trail when traveling from point A to point B. Then, hikers and dogs must camp at a designated AT shelter, either in the shelter or pitching a tent at the site. Every shelter has a bear box for storing food, cosmetics, and utensils. Some have a privy.

Dogs. Dogs must be on a leash no longer than 6 feet and under immediate control at all times. Dogs are not permitted in swimming areas or on designated swimming beaches. Dispose of pet waste responsibly. Dogs are not permitted on some state park trails, including at Cape May Point and Rancocas State Parks, due to the sensitivity of the areas—for example, where there are rare or endangered plant species and animal habitats. The Lake Nummy Trail in Belleplain State Forest does not allow dogs, but other trails exist at Belleplain for canine and human hiking. Additionally, some trails may become temporarily restricted. Call ahead to avoid disappointment.

The Division of Fish and Wildlife maintains 119 Wildlife Management Areas where your dog can romp leash free for seven months of the year. Of them, eleven contain dog-training areas that are open year-round. These are listed in Appendix B.

Other regulations. Some state parks and forests charge a parking fee from Memorial Day weekend through Labor Day weekend. Most also have hunting seasons. Check *www.njparksandforests.org* for fees and hunting schedules.

County and Township Park Systems

These parks are gems. Many are former estates. All have websites with contacts for information about regulations.

Of New Jersey's twenty-one counties, fourteen have off-leash dog parks where your dog can feel born free. They all have rules, which include maintaining control of your dog at all times and picking up after him. See Appendix A for a list.

New Jersey Conservation Foundation

The New Jersey Conservation Foundation preserves land and natural resources for the benefit of all, and its twenty-two preservation projects are open to the public for hiking. Although not all sites permit dogs, many do. Contact the foundation at (908) 234-1225 or *www.njconservation.org*.

Go Lightly on the Land

To borrow a phrase from Henry David Thoreau, I wish to speak a word for Nature. We go to the woods for an experience in quiet, beautiful nature—to commune, de-stress, and re-energize. And so does Fido, when you take him. After hiking several trails, you will see that the Garden State's parks and forests are true gifts to humans and dogs. Let us keep them clean and wild for all to enjoy, far into the future.

Leave No Trace is a national organization dedicated to educating people about reducing their impacts on the environment while enjoying it; conducting follow-up research on implemented techniques; and promoting ethical outdoors behavior. The seven original Leave No Trace principles were written for hiking in wilderness backcountry areas. We don't have quite the same concerns as in the West, however; the only wilderness backcountry in New Jersey is in the Pine Barrens. The principles can still be adapted to hiking with dogs in our densely populated, highly regulated landscape.

1. Plan ahead and prepare.

Know the regulations and special concerns for the area you'll visit. Prepare for extreme weather, hazards, and emergencies. Schedule your trip to avoid times of high use. Visit in small groups. Split larger parties into groups of four to six. Repackage food to minimize waste. Use a map and compass to eliminate the use of marking paint, rock cairns, or flagging.

In preparing for a hike with your canine pal, remember to do the same for Fido. Ask yourself these questions when appropriate: Is the dog healthy and able to hike rugged terrain? Are his paws calloused enough

Backpackers can spend the night in a shelter on the Appalachian Trail. At the Brinks shelter Lance makes dinner, while Farley ignores his.

to walk on rocks without getting ripped to shreds? Am I carrying enough food and water for me and my dog?

2. Travel and camp on durable surfaces.

Durable surfaces include established trails and campsites, rock, gravel, dry grasses, and snow. Protect riparian areas by camping at least 200 feet from lakes and streams. Good campsites are found, not made. Altering a site is unnecessary.

In popular areas:

- Concentrate use on existing trails and campsites.
- Walk single file in the middle of the trail, even when it is wet or muddy.
- Keep campsites small. Focus activity in areas where vegetation is absent.

3. Dispose of waste properly.

Pack it in; pack it out. Inspect your campsite and rest areas for trash or spilled foods. Pack out all trash, leftover food, and litter. Deposit solid human waste in cat holes dug 6 to 8 inches deep at least 200 feet away from water, camp, and trails. Cover and disguise the cat hole when finished. Pack out toilet paper and hygiene products. To wash yourself or your dishes, carry water 200 feet away from streams or lakes and use small amounts of biodegradable soap (or just use water and put utensils in "no mess" freezer bags to pack out). Scatter strained dishwater; pack out strained food particles.

Leave No Trace is studying the impact of hikers' waste in the Pine Barrens, New Jersey's most environmentally sensitive area, which sits on top of a huge aquifer. Because human waste is more damaging than pet waste, there is growing support in the movement for hikers to pack it all out.

4. Leave what you find.

Preserve the past. Examine but do not touch cultural or historic structures and artifacts. Leave rocks, plants, and other natural objects as you find them. Don't let your dog dig willy-nilly.

From Cape May to High Point, New Jersey's woods are full of history, and evidence abounds of the people who lived and worked there. Ruins of towns, factories, farms, mines, and even robbers' hangouts decorate the woods. Take a moment and reflect to feel their long-ago presence.

Along the Paulins Kill

Avoid introducing or transporting nonnative species. During warmer months be aware of where you have been in your hiking boots. In particular, be careful not to transport aquatic weeds that can invade and alter habitats. Check your boots and rinse them off after hiking in a wetland. Check that your dog is not carrying seeds in his fur.

5. Minimize campfire impacts.

Use a lightweight stove for cooking, and enjoy a candle lantern for light (or use a headlamp or flashlight). Where fires are permitted (private campgrounds only when hiking with your dog), use established fire rings. Keep fires small. Use only sticks from the ground that can be broken by hand. Burn all wood and coals to ash, put out campfires completely, then scatter cool ashes.

6. Respect wildlife.

Observe wildlife from a distance. Do not follow or approach wildlife. Never feed animals. Feeding wildlife damages their health, alters natural behaviors, and exposes them to predators and other dangers. Protect wildlife and your food by storing rations and trash securely. Control pets at all times, or leave them at home. Avoid wildlife during sensitive times, such as when they are mating, nesting, or raising young, and during winter.

7. Be considerate of other visitors.

Respect other visitors and protect the quality of their experiences. Be courteous. Yield to other users on the trail (and step aside). Let nature's sound prevail. Pick up dog droppings to reduce an animal's impact on other people.

Camp Care: Cleanup

After the tent is pitched and you are anticipating a good meal after hiking all day, the time for good housekeeping begins. It is essential to be meticulous while preparing food, eating, and cleaning up. Try to make only what you will eat, and try to use one pot. Get out your freezer bags, and pack out all trash and leftovers.

When cleaning the cooking pot, dish, cup, and utensils, use as little water as possible and scatter it at least 200 feet away from the campsite and stream. You do not want to attract bears or other wildlife to the tent or shelter, especially while you are sleeping. Some hardy folks drink the water and pot cleanings. Be sure to either pack cookware in the sack that you fling over the tree branch or put it in the bear box.

Feed your dog outside the shelter and after he has eaten, and make sure no pieces of dog food are left on the ground. Stash his bowl in the bear box, too.

Clean yourself and brush your teeth at least 200 feet away from any body of water. If you use soap, use as little as possible of an unscented, biodegradable soap. Better yet, use unscented body wipes, available online or through outdoors stores. Pack them home with you.

When you are ready to leave camp the next morning, take a last look around. Is the campsite just as clean, if not more so, than how you found it?

Gear for You and Your Dog

Proper hiking boots are the most important gear for people. Good boots should cover the ankle, lending support and guarding against twisting an ankle when hiking over New Jersey's rocky trails. Buy boots that weigh as little as possible. Go to a good outdoors store and try them on, as different brands fit differently. Most of the hikes in this book follow streams where flooding occurs or that require crossing, so waterproof boots are advised. Hiking in winter is impossible without them.

A good pair of cushiony, water-wicking hiking socks are more than just socks—they are tools. Your feet will be glad you invested.

On a short hike, a large fanny pack is sufficient, as long as it can hold at least two bottles of water and other essentials for you and your dog. Otherwise, carry a well-constructed day pack and practice the art of risk management when stuffing it: Make sure you have enough gear and supplies for the day's hike, plus more in case you get lost in the dark and have to spend the night in the woods. At least Bowser will keep you warm.

Light-colored clothing will make ticks easier to spot (see Getting Ready, this chapter). Think about wearing slicker fabrics in fall and spring, as ticks attach better to fabrics with fluffy surfaces, such as fleece.

Ten Essentials for Humans: A Systems Approach

1. **Navigation (map and compass).** Topo maps have a lot of interesting information that tells you where you are. Learn to use a compass and a GPS unit to really lock in your navigational skills. Sometimes equipment fails. To be safest, learn to tell time by looking at the sun,

not only your watch. It's easy and fun. Here's how: When you enter the woods, note the time and whether the sun is in front of you, behind you, or off to one side. Remember, the sun rises in the east and sets in the west. If the sun is directly overhead, it is noon. If the sun is at your back when you begin your hike in the morning, you are heading west, away from the rising sun. On your return, you will know to head east back to your car.

2. **Sun protection (sunglasses and sunscreen).** Current research questions whether vitamin D from the sun prevents more cancer than sunscreen does, but check with your doctor first. Bring a hat with a brim, and put a dab of sunscreen on your dog's nose.

3. **Insulation (extra clothing).** Bring enough to keep you warm at night, should you be in the woods. Make your clothes do double duty. Bring raingear that protects you from wind and provides an outer layer over an additional sweater or light jacket. During hunting season, wear a blaze orange hat or vest, available in sporting goods or outdoors stores.

4. **Illumination (headlamp or flashlight).** It gets dark in the forest quicker than you might think. If you lose your way or spend more time on the trail than you planned, you will need a light to see blazes and read your map. Check your batteries before you go.

5. **First-aid supplies.** Buy a kit from a camping store or make your own with bandages, aspirin, superglue, cold pack, antiseptic, adhesive, and tweezers.

6. **Fire (firestarter and matches/lighter).** Pack waterproof matches, lighters, and other firestarters in plastic bags. A fire is a good emergency signal if you are lost or injured.

7. **Repair kit and tools (including knife).** Multipurpose knife, duct tape, tiny sewing kit. You never know when you will need them.

8. **Nutrition (extra food).** Bring plenty of snacks, then pack extra. A short break on a big rock with a nice view and a tasty snack does wonders for energy levels. If you get lost and wander around more than you planned, you'll be glad you packed those extra goodies.

9. **Hydration (extra water).** Most essential. Always bring plenty of water. For an eight-hour day in warm weather, or a shorter day on a strenuous hike, pack 3 liters of water for you and 3 for a big dog. Bring a purification kit to use water from a stream. Some places, such as the Kittatinny Ridge, may have few or no fresh water sources, especially during dry summers.

10. **Emergency shelter.** Should you get lost or injured and darkness falls, a space blanket or space tent will help you and your dog through the night. They also can be handy if you are caught in storms.

Ten Essentials for Canines

1. **Obedience training.** New Jersey's leash laws, dense population, and tight spaces demand that your dog be well behaved. Before you set foot on a trail, make sure your dog is trained and can be trusted to behave when faced with other hikers, dogs, wildlife, or strange scents and sights.

2. **Doggy backpack.** Let your dog carry his own gear. Most doggy packs are made with high-tech materials such as Cordura with ballistic nylon and padded with fleece or canvas-lined coated pack cloth. Check that packs are reinforced in areas that might scrape against rocks, have reflective areas for night hiking, and are padded for a comfortable fit. Comfort is most important; proper placement is over the shoulders, not directly over the back. Bright-colored packs make your dog more visible during hunting season or if lost.

3. **Basic first-aid kit.** See A Doggy First-Aid Kit, this chapter.

4. **Dog food and trail treats.** Keep Bowser extra well fed on the trail since he will burn more calories than usual. Bring extra snacks in case you get lost and spend the night in the woods. On overnight backpack trips, bring his regular food and plenty of snacks in case he stops eating, as some dogs do their first time out. If he stops eating dog food and doggy snacks, be prepared to share your own food. If he stops eating altogether, he should be fine for a few days as long as he drinks water. Trail treats give quick energy on a strenuous day of hiking. Train your dog to carry his own food and water.

5. **Water and water bowl.** Don't count on finding water along the trail. Pack enough for the entire day. You may want to substitute Gatorade or Pedialyte for one bottle of water, but try these products out on your dog ahead of time. A good rule of thumb is 3 liters of water for Fido's day hike. If he is hot or thirsty and all your water is gone and you do not have a purification kit, use uncommon good sense about letting him drink from a stream. Measure the risk—heatstroke that could result in death versus possible intestinal parasites that can be treated with antibiotics. Bring a lightweight plastic or titanium bowl or buy a foldable doggy bowl. Offer your dog water when he looks thirsty and every time that you have a drink. Use your own thirst

Petey carries his own food and water bowls in his padded pack for an overnight hike on the AT.

level as a guide to know when your dog might be thirsty. Do not use a water bladder for yourself unless you have trained Fido to use one also. People tend to sip almost inadvertently, unaware of whether or not they are truly thirsty, when using a water bladder. They may also be unaware of their dogs' thirst, which may lead to dehydration and heatstroke. Use your own thirst, as well as a keen eye, to gauge Fido's thirst. Water bladders are available for dogs, but train him to use one at home.

6. **Leash and collar.** In New Jersey, it's the law. Most parks require leashes that are a maximum of 6 feet long. Nylon or leather is comfortable and adequate for easy control. Retractable leashes are not recommended as dogs may get too far away from you and easily get into trouble. Keep your dog close. Harnesses do not provide the control that collars do. During hunting season, arm your dog with a wide, blaze orange collar or doggy vest so he is easily seen. Buy it in a sporting goods store or online.

7. **Insect repellent.** Some animals, like people, have negative reactions to DEET-based repellents. So, before leaving home, dab a little DEET-based repellent on a patch of your dog's fur to see if he reacts to it. Look for signs of drowsiness, lethargy, and/or nausea. Restrict repellent applications to those places the dog can't lick—the back of the neck and around the ears, staying clear of ears and inner ears. Try natural repellents, too. Soak a cotton ball in a natural oil, wrap it in a bandana, and tie it around your dog's neck before you hit the trail.

8. **ID tags and picture identification.** Don't worry; be happy and make sure Fido is properly identified should he become separated from you. Get him microchipped and give him a nice, shiny identification tag to wear. Nearly all shelters and police now have scanners to read a microchip, a grain-size transponder with its very own code for your dog's permanent identification. A veterinarian injects the chip under the loose skin at the dog's shoulders. You register the transponder with the American Kennel Club. ID tags are a fast, easy read for anyone. Why take chances? Do both. Put a photograph of your dog in your pack. If he gets lost, make flyers from the picture to post in nearby communities.

9. **Dog booties.** Booties can be used to keep bandages secure if the dog damages his pads or to protect against snowballs between the toes that melt, freeze, and cut, causing lameness. Choose booties that allow the dog's toenails to stick out through the front so he is able to grip trail surfaces. Because a dog sweats through his pads, some booties, which are available in many materials and styles, can prevent sweating and interrupt the dog's ability to cool down, especially on warm days. "Vet wrap" helps keep booties in place.

10. **Plastic bags and trowel.** Be courteous and leave the trail as you found it. Keep people loving dogs by carrying out your dog's waste in places that require it. On other trails, dig a hole and bury it.

You may want to bring two more comfort items for your favorite hiking buddy. If you hike on days with a chance of showers or on overnight or backpack trips, why not stash a rain jacket for Spike in his pack? It will keep him both warm and dry. In cold weather, short-haired dogs in particular need a jacket. On an overnight trip, be kind to your dog who has been sleeping in the house just like you. Bring a sleeping pad or blanket for him to sleep on so he can stave off the cold. Keep your dog leashed in your tent or close beside you in a shelter.

Sunshine, 12 years old, enjoys weight-bearing exercises while she hikes.

Health and Fitness Concerns for Your Dog

Many people think that a dog can just up and hike for hours because he is an animal. How wrong they are! And how miserable for an unsuspecting Spike! Imagine yourself after a sedentary life, or season, of lying in front of the fire and eating. Would you be ready to hike uphill for two hours?

Your dog gets tired, winded, and sore just like you do. To safely get your dog in shape just follow the Golden Rule: Do unto Spike as you would do unto yourself. Here are a few tips to help prepare him for a fun time hiking.

Getting Ready

Acclimate to temperature. Acclimate your dog to hot or cold weather before you venture out on a long hike. Start with short, local hikes and build up the time you spend outdoors in temperature extremes.

Backpack training. Start backpack training a dog as young as possible, first with a towel and then an empty pack. Build up the weight in the pack, distributing it evenly on both sides of the dog. A mature, two-year-old dog can carry up to 25 percent of his weight, and a few dogs are able to carry more.

Fitness program. Dogs have muscles, just like people, and they get fat, just like people. Put yourself and your dog on a fitness program together. Start with an easy walk in the park—but then, why not do it on a trail?

But, Ma, Daddy lets me take a mud bath!

Choose an easy hike on a flat trail with a few access points so you can create a hike at your endurance level. Flat trails and trails with gentle hills are everywhere, even in the Highlands and Ridge and Valley—New Jersey's highest, most rugged terrain. Build up to a few miles, then hit the hills. Get moving!

Little dogs. Little guys can go places big ones can't. Build up your back muscles and throw Spikelet in a pack while you climb those long rock slabs. He eats and weighs next to nothing.

Tiny critters. Deer ticks infected with Lyme disease–causing bacteria are everywhere in New Jersey, and they are difficult to spot crawling through a dog's coat. But you can protect your favorite hiking buddy. Talk to your vet about a killed Lyme vaccine. Most dogs tolerate it well, except for those with compromised immune systems.

Other defenses include chemical, herbal, or natural oil repellents. Eucalyptus, citronella, and tea tree are a few commonly used oils. Soak a cotton ball with an oil of your choosing, wrap the cotton in a bandana, and tie it around your dog's neck.

Mosquitoes can cause heartworm, and infection rates from particular regions are generally unknown. To protect your dog, put him on heartworm-prevention medication, especially if you hike in a wide variety of areas or around a lot of water.

Rabies occurs in some locations more than others. Don't approach wildlife, especially strange-acting wildlife. Rabies takes two forms in wildlife: a furious form and a dumb form. If you see a skunk, raccoon, or possum in the daytime, stay away! Stay up-to-date on your dog's rabies shots. Don't take chances—protect your four-legged friend.

Older dogs. Keep older dogs with stiff joints and arthritis off difficult trails and any that require rock scrambling or climbing. Stick to short hikes on gentle hills and flat terrain.

When backpacking and camping, give your old hiking buddy something soft to lie on. Pack a sleeping bag liner or pad just for him. Dogs age at different rates—the bigger the dog, the faster he ages. A small thirteen-year-old dog may be the equivalent of sixty-eight in human years, but a big guy can be one hundred. If your dog is unable to walk anymore, make a litter and drag him out. Use good judgment and don't take a dog farther than is safe for his age and fitness level.

Pads. Toughen them up! Check your dog's pads to determine whether the central pad has a thick callous for good protection. Outside dogs and some breeds have a lot of keratin and naturally tough pads. If you need to toughen up your dog's pads, do exactly what you would do for your own feet if you were barefoot—start with slow, short hikes to toughen them up. Take your dog for hikes on roads and rail trails before you hit the high, rocky trails. Initially, if a road is too hot for you to walk on barefoot, then it is too hot for your dog. As you graduate to longer hikes and more rugged terrain, check your dog's pads every 2 or 3 miles. It takes a long time for a dog's pads to get tough.

Puppies. Puppies need a rabies shot before hitting the trail. Some veterinarians don't recommend taking a pup hiking until he is at least six months old and has had all his vaccinations. Talk to your vet to find out when your pup is ready to hike.

Teaching Spike to enjoy water. Getting used to sitting or lying in water can save your dog's life if he gets overheated on a warm weather hike. To teach him, take him to a shallow stream where you can easily step in. Encourage him to walk in the water with you, but don't force him or make it a bad experience. If he takes one step in, praise him. If he steps out, don't say anything. Eventually, your dog will enjoy the sensation and look for water.

Are you in shape? Get out and hike with your dog. You will automatically get in better physical condition while having fun with your dog. There are plenty of "no excuses" hikes in this book to get you started.

When to Cut a Hike Short

Watch for a dramatic change in Spike's speed and enthusiasm. If he starts out walking with you and a mile down the trail he is lagging behind and must be coaxed to keep up, it is time to call it quits. The key is to know your dog! And remember the Golden Rule.

Canine First Aid

Anything can happen on the trail—encounters with wildlife, bee stings, and torn dewclaws, diarrhea, heatstroke and hypothermia, snakebite, and exposure to toxins. When hiking with your dog, it is wise to be prepared.

Bee stings. Give your dog 25 milligrams of Benadryl, an antihistamine. If you can find the sting spot, apply ammonia or baking soda, which, being alkaline, neutralizes the acid from the stinger and allows you to take the stinger out. Dogs usually get stung on the face, so watch for a local reaction such as a fat lip. If your dog has no respiratory distress, Benadryl alone is fine. Some dogs are allergic to bee stings, as are people. Should you decide to take your allergic dog out hiking, always carry an EpiPen, an instant emergency measure obtained from your veterinarian.

Cuts and torn dewclaws and toenails. Clean the wound with hydrogen peroxide and then water. Control the bleeding by applying pressure or blood-stop powder or hemostatic powder. Apply superglue while holding the wound together. Minor cuts can be helped with an alum stick.

Diarrhea. Give the dog Kaopectate caplets or tablets.

Heat and heatstroke. Recognize signs of heatstroke: disorientation, glazed eyes, staggering, flopping down in a prostrate position and not moving, tongue hanging out longer than usual, red gums, dry mouth. A dog's tongue is his cooling system. If his mouth is dry, his moisture level is evaporating. Act quickly, heatstroke can be life threatening.

Get the dog's core temperature down. Find water—a pond or a stream—and lay him in it to transfer the heat from the dog's body into the water. This is better than anything else you can do. Give him Gatorade or Pedialyte to replenish electrolytes. Buffered aspirin and a cold-water enema with a syringe also help drop temperature. Rest until your dog has recuperated enough to leave the trail. Always know where water is in relation to your hike.

Dogs with thick undercoats do not tolerate heat well because there is little capillary cooling through the surface of their skin. Dogs who have shed out their undercoats, even those with long hair such as golden retrievers, do better in warmer temperatures. If you notice your dog is getting hot while hiking on dry upland away from a stream, periodically pour bottled water onto your dog's topline and rub it in to help keep him cool.

Opposite: Farley takes a break on the Primrose Brook Trail in Jockey Hollow.

Hypothermia. It is unlikely, but possible, for a dog to succumb to hypothermia in New Jersey. In extremely cold temperatures, or if your dog gets wet to the skin in icy water, he can lose his normal body temperature to the surrounding cold air. To protect the dog's core, blood stops circulating to the extremities and limbs begin to freeze. Check body parts suffering from hypothermia first. Feel the tips of ears for swelling and soreness. Webs between the toes lose their pink color and light-colored pads discolor to reddish-purple from uncirculating blood. Look for soreness and uniform swelling across and between the toes. And be aware that as body temperature goes down, a dog becomes sleepy.

Raise the dog's core temperature slowly and then get him moving. Use your own body to warm his if you can. Massage his ears or toes with your hand back to 101° F, slightly warmer than you are. Crush heat packs and put them under the dog's armpits, areas rich in blood supply. Try using a gradient solution of water, each dose slightly warmer than the last, but be careful—a wet dog can lose heat fast. Put a solar blanket around him.

Protect your dog from losing more heat by wrapping his feet with booties, bandages, or your extra pair of gloves. If he is too lame to walk, make a litter and carry him out.

Prevention is key. Leave your dog with circulatory problems at home on cold winter days or just go out for a short walk and keep him moving.

Torn, frozen, or bleeding pads. Carry dog booties, but be careful when you use them. When a dog lacerates his pads on really sharp rocks, he still needs his feet to get off the trail. If his pads bleed, follow the instructions under Cuts and Torn Dewclaws and Toenails and then use the booties. When it warrants, use plastic sandwich bags to waterproof his feet. (Turn used sandwich bags inside out.) Booties and bags are better than applying petroleum jelly or baby oil, which attract and hold debris to the foot.

When hiking in snow, watch for icy snow that can cut your dog's pads. If you find yourself on ice, prevent an accident by holding the leash tight to keep him close.

Pain, arthritis. Give buffered aspirin—a low dose of 81 milligrams to dogs 50 pounds and up. Give half that amount to a smaller dog. Dogs can tolerate ibuprofen, but always give it with food. Do not give Tylenol!

Poison ivy. Spike can be a carrier of poison ivy toxins when the plant brushes against his coat. If you are allergic, refrain from hugging him until you clean him off. Rub loose soil all over him to soak up the plant's oils, then wash the soil off in a stream.

Sprains. Use cold packs twenty minutes on and twenty minutes off to control swelling.

Snakebite. Get off the trail and get the dog to a veterinarian immediately. If the dog was bitten on a leg, restrict his movements by applying a very snug bandage that covers the length of the leg. Put the dog on a litter and carry him off the trail. Antivenin to carry with you can be obtained from a veterinarian, but it is expensive and has a short shelf life.

Most snakebites occur on the face. The best defense is prevention. Always know where your dog is and don't let him stick his face in a hole. Would you stick your own face in a hole? Remember the Golden Rule.

Sunburn. Prevent sunburn on your light-skinned dog's nose by using sunscreen.

Toxins. Toxins that may be encountered on a hike include everything from antifreeze in parking lot puddles to chocolate, drugs, a sock, plants, and discarded waste of various kinds. First, decide whether you want your dog to regurgitate the toxin out of his system. If he swallowed a caustic substance or a sharp object, it might not be wise to bring it up through his esophagus. Give him activated charcoal to neutralize toxins, then take him off the trail and to a veterinarian immediately. If he swallowed a foreign object, drugs, or a plant, give him a good dose of hydrogen peroxide

Chicken 'shroom (Laetiporous sulphureus) *on Kittatiny Mountain*

A Doggy First-Aid Kit

A doggy first-aid kit is necessary, even with only the bare essentials. For a comprehensive canine first-aid kit when heading into the wild with your dog, pack the following essentials:

Instruments
- Scissors/bandage scissors/toenail clippers
- Rectal thermometer (a healthy dog has a rectal temperature of 101°F)

Cleansers and disinfectants
- 3% hydrogen peroxide
- Betadine
- Canine eyewash, available at pet supply stores

Topical antibiotics and ointments
- Calamine lotion
- Triple antibiotic ointment (Bacitracin, Neomycin, or Polymyxin)
- Baking soda (for bee stings)
- Petroleum jelly
- Stop-bleeding powder

Medications
- Enteric-coated aspirin or Bufferin
- Imodium-AD
- Pepto-Bismol

Dressings and bandages
- Gauze pads (4-inch square) or gauze roll
- Nonstick pads
- Adhesive tape (1-inch and 2-inch rolls)

Miscellaneous
- Muzzle
- Dog booties
- Any prescription medication your dog needs

For extended trips
Consult your vet about any other prescription medications that may be needed in emergency situations, including:
- Oral antibiotics
- Eye/ear medications
- Emetics (to induce vomiting)
- Pain medications and anti-inflammatories
- Suturing materials for large open wounds

Extra items

- Alum stick or styptic pencil—stops minor capillary bleeding
- Benadryl
- Charcoal, activated
- Chemical cold and heat packs
- Hemostatic powder
- Kaopectate
- Moleskin
- Pantyhose to use as a muzzle
- Solar blanket
- Syringe, plastic
- Superglue
- Thermometer, rectal, plastic digital
- Tweezers
- Vet wrap

Doc Tallamy examines Tank.

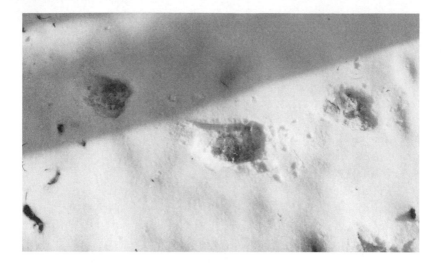

Seeing signs of forest inhabitants, like these bear tracks at Norvin Green State Forest, is a benefit of winter hiking.

Wildlife

Bears and coyotes have been seen in all twenty-one counties of the state, with the heaviest concentration of bears in Warren, Sussex, Passaic, and Morris Counties. It is a rare event to see a bear south of Trenton. As long as your dog is on a leash when hiking and camping, there is no need to fear a bear or coyote. A dog is a benefit to alert the hiker, and a barking dog may also cause the bear to wander off.

Bears: Most black bears will turn and go away from you before you ever know they are there. But the increased population of black bears in the state, combined with their lessening fear of humans and knowledge that humans bring food, means it is wise to be alert. Your dog will usually spot a bear before you do, so let him be your safely tethered scout in bear country.

If you do see a bear on the trail, especially a sow with cubs, make a lot of noise while looking for a big stick to bang on trees. Do not run! The idea is to seem larger than the average bear. If the bear advances in your direction, get more aggressive and throw rocks, blow a whistle or air horn, wave hands, beat a stick on trees, and yell or back up slowly, still making noise, and leave. Never look the bear in the eyes, which it interprets as a challenge. A bear that gets within 10 feet of a person should be considered aggressive. Get ready to hit it on the snout with your stick.

Never let your dog chase a bear, for no size dog can scare a bear. Most attacks on dogs are provoked when an owner lets his dog loose to chase a bear. And if a bear does attack a dog, it is because the bear is going to eat it. Do not let Spike off the leash, even at night when you are all sleeping in a tent. If he needs to go out during the night, take him out on the leash so there is no chance of anything happening.

Under normal situations in the woods, there is little need to worry, but it is always a good idea to check with park personnel about any bear activity before you hike. And don't pack tuna fish sandwiches or salads; they are especially strong smelling and therefore attractive to bears.

Coyotes: Coyotes hunt in family groups and communicate by howling, so you may hear them in the night. They rarely attack dogs, but if a dog chases a coyote, a running coyote may turn around to fight the dog. Do not let your dog chase a coyote.

Snakes: Two upland venomous snakes live in New Jersey: the state-endangered timber rattlesnake and the northern copperhead. Both are timid creatures and would rather move away from people when they feel threatened, so give them room to do so. Chances are slim that you will see one in your open line of sight on the trail. They lie under blueberry and other bushes and are almost impossible to see—good reason to stay on the trail.

Dogs and people get bitten by a snake when they accidentally step on one, or when a dog sticks his face into a hole. Rattlesnakes hide behind logs and rocks in wait for small rodents, their prey. Copperheads go to moist, grassy areas to feed on frogs and tend to lurk in stone walls where chipmunks travel.

Timber rattlesnakes and northern copperheads have hemotoxic venom that runs through the prey's circulatory system and slowly begins to digest the organs. The good news is that you have time to get help. Most people don't know if they are allergic to the venom, which can cause anaphylactic shock. The best thing to do if you get bitten when hiking is to tell the first person you see and ask them to come with you to the hospital. If you have an allergic reaction, that person can at least speak for you. It has become the new practice for hospitals not to give antivenin right away. Instead, they monitor the person, hoping that his or her body will combat the toxin on its own.

Dogs are different. Some small ones have survived bites, and large ones have died. Prevention is key. Keep your dog on a leash and on the trail, with his nose where it belongs.

Hiking in Snake Country
- Don't step on teetering rocks.
- Don't put your hands down for leverage if you fall.
- If you fall, bounce right back up.
- When stepping over a log, look to the other side first for a little head sticking up.

Weather

Excessive heat, cold, ice, and deep snow are all signs to keep your dog indoors. Whether or not to hike in temperature extremes also depends on the dog's condition, age, and health. If the temperature and humidity added together equal 150, keep your dog home.

Generally, heavy-coated and large dogs are more susceptible to heat-stroke than shorter-haired and smaller dogs. With a body temperature that starts at 101°F, our canine pals are always warmer than us. If you're hot, they're hotter. In extremely hot and humid weather, think about what happens to an asthmatic dog's respiratory and cardiovascular systems. What are the pollen and mold counts? How about days with broadcast warnings to stay indoors? Remember the Golden Rule: Do unto Spike as you would do unto yourself.

At the cold end of the thermometer, ask yourself if your dog is used to walking in snow or below-freezing temperatures for a long time. Can he handle snowballs between his toes? Consider his weight and condition.

Winter hiking is wonderful. Leafless trees create great views, and the mountains can block the wind. Temperatures in the high 20s to 50s keep you just warm enough. Be sure to start out early in the day to allow plenty of time for lollygagging and the possibility of getting lost. You do not want to get caught by the early darkness out in the woods in below-freezing temperatures.

If you get caught in a thunderstorm, move to lower ground and crouch with as little of your body touching the ground as possible. Throw your rain jacket, stashed in your day pack, over you and your dog. There is nothing to do but wait out the storm.

Hunting Season Safety

Most state lands and many county and township parks allow hunting in the fall and winter. Check their websites or call to make sure of dates. New Jersey does not permit hunting on Sundays, except on private land. This writer has hiked often and alone during hunting season without problems.

A visitor at Watchung Reservation makes a new canine friend.

To be safe, wear a blaze orange vest or cap, and buy a vest for Bowser, too, especially if he is large and brown. Search online pet suppliers.

Using This Book

This guidebook describes some fun trails for you and your dog to enjoy, but remember that trails can change. They may be rerouted to give eroded paths a chance to heal; a footbridge may be wiped out by a storm. At the Delaware Water Gap National Recreation Area, a whole section of trail—bridges, streambed, and banks—was washed out by a hurricane, and it took a long time to reroute and rebuild it. Sometimes trails are closed due to nesting birds or other wildlife needs. It is always a good idea to call to check on conditions before you go. Phone numbers and websites are listed with each hike.

Most hikes in this book are loops, but most distances are given as a round-trip, which represents the actual hiking mileage. Two overnight hikes on the Appalachian Trail are given as one-way and require two cars.

The elevation range tells you how much of a climb you will have, although no particular gear or clothing is needed to reach New Jersey's highest summits.

Hike difficulty is based on an average weekend or monthly hiker and may be over- or underrated, depending on your fitness level. Easy hikes have elevations gains of 100 feet or less. Some are higher with gentle climbs or shorter distances, and a few flat, long-distance trails have many places to exit. All easy hikes require little exertion and are easy on the leg muscles. Moderate hikes have elevation gains of 190 to 1100 feet with many ups and downs, as is characteristic of the Highlands. Some have a steep ascent or descent. One flat hike has no quick exit. Moderate hikes are fun cardio workouts. Difficult hikes have steeper or more ascents and descents and are heavier cardio workouts.

Hiking time is based on an average walking speed of 2 miles per hour. The terrain and condition of you and your dog may alter this. The best canine hiking season takes into account temperatures, terrain, and precipitation, as well as tick feeding seasons in particularly strong tick habitats. Regulations and contact information for land managers are given so you have access to all information about an area you want to hike in. All known map sources are listed.

Dr. Paul Tallamy, a licensed veterinarian at Green Valley Veterinary Clinic, shared his knowledge for the sections on Canine First Aid and Health and Fitness Concerns for Your Dog. Talk with your own veterinarian about your dog's health concerns and whether your dog is ready to hit the trail.

Lance L. Casper, owner of Muddy Foot Farm, shared his knowledge of basic obedience in Canine Trail Etiquette. He has bred and trained hunting dogs and dogs with special problems for more than thirty years.

Larry Herrighty, senior wildlife biologist with the New Jersey Department of Environmental Protection (NJDEP), offered his expertise and advice about interacting with wildlife.

For the Novice: A Word About Trail Blazes

Most state and federal lands use traditional methods for blazing trails: Three blazes denote the start and end of a trail; two blazes indicate a turn with the topmost blaze pointing in the direction the trail turns; and one blaze tells you that you are on the trail. If you think you have gotten off the trail and don't see a blaze ahead of you, turn around and look for a blaze behind you (meant to direct folks coming from the other direction). If you do not see one, go back the way you came until you do see one. Then figure it out.

In fall when leaves cover the ground, the path itself may be impossible to see. Always look for blazes in front of you and behind you. They may be on rocks, trees, or posts.

Do not turn onto a side trail unless a blaze that you are looking for tells you to do so. If you are unsure, stay on your path; do not turn.

How the Trails Were Selected

New Jersey is a state of drama. It is the most densely populated state in the country; yet, its landscape is incredibly diverse. It is ancient and eroded, with glacially sculpted and volcanic mountains formed by crashing continents, and it has been covered by oceans many times. It has karst topography with limestone sinkholes, great valleys and wild ridges, Wild and Scenic Rivers, the most famous footpath in the world, ocean beaches, swamps on mountaintops and lowlands, a pygmy pine forest, a 17-trillion-gallon freshwater aquifer, and a United Nations–designated biosphere.

Given this small state's complex topography and geologic history, every twist of the path will bring you and Spike to something new—a glacial lake, rock scramble, breezy outcrop, stream to cross, or different habitat, critters, and landforms. Every trail selected for this book has something outstanding to offer you and your dog on a hike. Trails from all five physiographic regions are represented here for every level of dog and human hiker, no matter what shape you both are in.

The two coastal plains cover 60 percent of the land in New Jersey. There, short, flat trails are easy and fun—perfect for beginning hikers. You and your dog will feel like you're walking on air as you hike the cuestas that separate the inner and outer coastal plains. Then surprisingly hilly terrain occurs in Hartshorne Woods in the Highlands of the Navesink. Your feet will feel massaged and almost bounce from the paths. Rack up a few hours or all day on the sandy flats or beach where even experienced hikers can get a real workout.

In the Piedmont's central lowlands, which cover 20 percent of New Jersey, flat, easy towpaths stretch from Milford to New Brunswick. You and your dog will revel in the rolling terrain and low ridges that offer a hint of rigor. Do 5 or 6 miles in the Watchungs, and you will both be ready for the Highlands mountains and Kittatinny Ridge.

More experienced dogs and humans can hit the massive, broad ridges of the Highlands region, which covers 12 percent of the state. Novice and expert hikers alike will want to sashay and sniff along floriferous streams than run through the foothills and valley.

Kittatinny Mountain spreads across the northwestern Ridge and Valley region, which covers 8.5 percent of New Jersey. Its rock outcrops, glacial lakes, splashing waterfalls, views, climbs, and fertile valleys are well worth an experienced dog's effort. Everyone, no matter what your condition, can enjoy a hike on the lengthy rail trails that cross Kittatinny Valley.

The Appalachian National Scenic Trail runs along the mountain ridge, then slides down into the Kittatinny Valley.

Some criteria for choosing the trails in this book include:

- Streams, lakes, waterfalls along route
- Shade for much of the hike
- Water en route to cool a warm or hot dog, if needed
- Minimal contact with livestock and horses
- Loop route
- Interesting and variable terrain
- Easy accessibility
- Variety for all levels of experience in all areas of the state

There are easy, moderate, and difficult hikes in every section. Pick one!

Choosing a Trail

If you and your dog are over age forty-five, or if hiking is new to you or Spike, start gently. Choose a local trail and go farther as your addiction to the great outdoors grabs hold. Then head a little south, switching between flat trails, the beach, and the foot-massaging hills of the coastal plain parks, such as those in Monmouth County. You both will build up a healthy addiction in no time, but just in time to hit the volcanic mini-mountains that comprise the Watchungs, then the rocky rubble of the Highlands, the eroded jutting ridges of Kittatinny Mountain, and the long sand roads of the Pine Barrens—New Jersey's wild places. Flat trails exist in all of the Garden State's physiographic regions, and old woods roads appear just about everywhere. These roads were built for a multitude of purposes, including logging, farming, mining, carriage travel, and war.

In warm weather, choose a hike that runs close to a stream and go wading with your dog—on leash, of course! In fall, head high to see the blazing colors of the Garden State's mixed-hardwood forests with views across valleys. In spring, don't miss the waterfalls.

Be wise, and hike with a human buddy in addition to your canine friend, especially on the northern rocky mountain trails. But go, if you must, alone with Bowser on the more central and southern flat trails. Just tell someone where you're going.

Get Involved

Ever wonder who takes care of trails and puts stepping-stones and boards across wet areas and builds bridges over streams? Or who carried all that lumber up a hillside to make steps? The answer is mostly volunteers and park personnel. But the fact is, funds are tight and paid employees have other duties as well. Most parks rely on volunteers to spend a day on some regular basis clipping shrubs, removing trash, reconstructing washed-out bridges, painting blazes, and doing whatever is necessary to keep trails open and enjoyable.

Those who hike the trails from Morris County on north are fortunate, for the well-organized New York–New Jersey Trail Conference (NY-NJTC) volunteers help maintain many trails on federal, state, and county lands there. This federation of more than one hundred hiking clubs and ten thousand individuals is dedicated to building and maintaining marked trails. They are always looking for more volunteers to join their crews. Contact them at (201) 512-9348 or *www.nynjtc.org.*

Views make strenuous climbs worthwhile. In some places, views have disappeared as trees grow and block them. It is unfortunate, but taking down these trees is not a priority for many parks lacking in the funds and personnel to do it. It is worth asking if they will allow volunteers to recreate the views that once helped give a park its natural glamour.

Parks in the central and southern parts of the state, outside the reach of the NY-NJTC volunteers, are less fortunate. This is sometimes reflected in overgrown trails and broken boardwalks. The Batona Hiking Club of Philadelphia helps maintain trails on state lands in south Jersey. Contact them at *members.aol.com/Batona* or Batona, 215 S. Spring Mill Road, Villanova, PA 19085-1409. Other hiking clubs may adopt trails or volunteer to build or maintain trails. You can find them on the Internet or on the NY-NJTC website, which lists hiking clubs and member organizations. Most parks—state, county, or township—have an "Adopt-A-Trail" program or schedule cleanup days. If not listed among the many trails in this book, find their phone numbers on the Internet. They will welcome your call.

Most parks run nature programs, hikes, and some type of outreach. Think about volunteering to lead hikes—maybe with your dog!—or help out with programs. Perhaps suggest a "Good Dog on the Trail" program.

Volunteer. Get involved. Spike will be happier for it too. Be a good dog ambassador.

Let's hike!

A Note About Safety

Safety is an important concern in all outdoor activities. No guidebook can alert you to every hazard or anticipate the limitations of every reader. Therefore, the descriptions of roads, trails, routes, and natural features in this book are not representations that a particular place or excursion will be safe for your party. When you follow any of the routes described in this book, you assume responsibility for your own safety. Under normal conditions, such excursions require the usual attention to traffic, road and trail conditions, weather, terrain, the capabilities of your party, and other factors. Keeping informed on current conditions and exercising common sense are the keys to a safe, enjoyable outing.

The Mountaineers Books

PART 2

The Trails

THE NORTHWEST RIDGE AND VALLEY

About 500 million years ago, the Proto-Atlantic Ocean covered New Jersey, depositing many layers of sediments. After millions of years, the ocean retreated. The sandstone and limestone became exposed and uplifted as mountains began to form.

When North America collided and became one with Africa and Europe, the mountains of New Jersey and along the rest of the East Coast crumpled upward, folding layers of rock to form the Appalachian Mountains.

Over millions of years, the softer sediments eroded. Streams cut through the harder rock, carrying the sediments away and leaving a valley through Sussex and Warren Counties, a 40-by-12-mile section of the United States Great Valley that stretches from Canada to the South.

Since about 700,000 years ago, three glaciers swept over the Ridge and Valley, dumping rocks and boulders from farther north, gouging out glacial lakes, creating streams and blocking others, smoothing rock formations, and generally altering the landscape into a varied terrain and habitat.

Different rocks broke down into different soil types that grew plants that preferred those characteristics. Streams, altitude, orientation to sun, and sometimes just an available spot where no other plant could grow fostered different habitats shared by particular animals, insects, and plants.

Today, bears and coyotes live in the fertile valley and mountainous forest expanses. Eastern timber rattlers den and bask on sun-baked rock outcrops, and raptors sail the ridge, searching the valley for prey. Streams with native trout run fast over the rocky land.

On the ridge's outcrops, stunted and twisted pitch pines grow with scrub oaks and grasses. Blueberry and huckleberry ripen in late summer, but—please!—leave some for the bears! In ravines and on northern exposures, eastern hemlock, spring-blooming rhododendron, and mountain laurel comprise the forest.

In the valley, railroads once carried passengers to resorts and also transported goods. Now the rail beds are rail trails in state parks, perfect for hiking. The Kittatinny Ridge offers a good climb to glorious views of the Great Valley and the Delaware River Valley. And, of course, the Appalachian National Scenic Trail runs the Kittatinny Ridge, across the valley and into the Highlands for 60.5 miles before entering New York.

Human and canine hikers alike will find plenty to keep them occupied on these lands, now federal and state parks, forests, and wildlife refuge.

1. Stepping-Stone Trail

Round-trip: 1.5 miles
Elevation range: 700–800 feet
Difficulty: Easy
Hiking time: 1 hour
Best canine hiking season: Fall, winter, spring
Regulations: Dogs must be leashed; day fee from Memorial Day
   weekend through Labor Day
Map: USGS Culvers Gap, NJ quadrangle
Information: Stokes State Forest, (973) 948-3820,
   www.njparksandforests.org

Getting there: Take US Highway 206 north to Stokes State Forest north of Branchville and just past Culvers Gap. Look for the Stokes State Forest sign, then turn right to enter the forest at the park office. After going through the gate, continue straight onto Coursen Road. Drive to the stop sign and turn left onto Kittle Road and then immediately left into the parking lot.

The Stepping-Stone Trail parallels a ravine where Stony Brook bounces over stepped waterfalls. The path descends gently through a hemlock forest to a clearing with two barns that were part of the Snook Lumber Mill and Dam circa 1800. The trail does not appear on any map, although it is

Petey watches Stony Brook cascade by the Stepping-Stone Trail.

easily found and followed. Its quiet drama creates a peaceful and distant feeling, as though you and your dog are very far from the crowds.

This trail is especially beautiful in snow when the hemlock and mountain laurel stand sharply against the land, and the edges of the Stony Brook crystallize as it rushes over slabs of red sandstone on its way to the Big Flat Brook.

Spike will love the sounds and scents of wildlife here—coyote, fox, deer, porcupine, and a lot of little critters. Being on leash keeps all four-legged animals safe. In winter, animal tracks are readily seen in the un-trampled snow for a fascinating glimpse of life in the forest.

From the lot, cross the street, walk through the picnic area and pick up the red-dot Silver Mine Trail, an old logging road, just after crossing Stony Brook. The path is wide, descending through hemlock and decidu-ous woods with splashes of young mountain laurel.

Soon the brook catches up to the trail and spills over the first falls. There, the Silver Mine Trail turns right into the woods but you go straight ahead on this unmarked old road, now the Stepping-Stone Trail. Go off the trail down to the stream where, in warm weather, its quieter pools are perfect places for Spike to take a dip on a long leash. Skinny streams flow from the hillside and cross the trail down to the brook. The path narrows first as a ledge between hillside and cliff, then through hardwoods, open shrubby fields, and a pond. There are a lot of different habitats for you and your dog along this exciting path. Come back the same way.

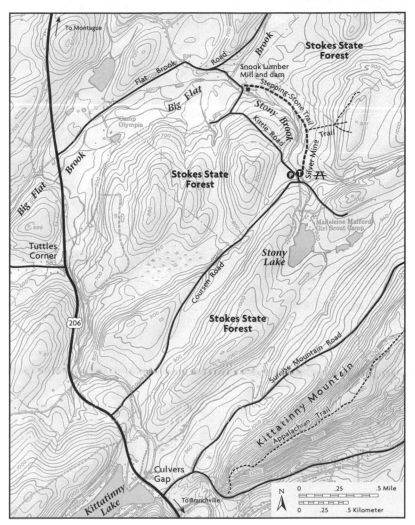

2. Sunrise Mountain Road Loop

Round-trip: 3.4 miles
Elevation range: 1000–1300 feet
Difficulty: Moderate
Hiking time: 2.5 hours
Best canine hiking season: Spring, summer, fall
Regulations: Dogs must be leashed

Maps: USGS Branchville, NJ quadrangle; NY-NJTC Kittatinny Trails
Map 18; NJDEP Stokes State Forest
Information: Stokes State Forest, (973) 948-3820,
www.njparksandforests.org

Getting there: Take US Highway 206 North to Stokes State Forest. Turn
right onto Upper North Shore Road (County Road 636) for about 100
yards and then turn left onto Sunrise Mountain Road. Drive 4 miles, passing the turnoff to Sunrise Mountain, and park at the Howell Trailhead
on the right. Sunrise Mountain Road is closed from the second week in
December to approximately April 1.

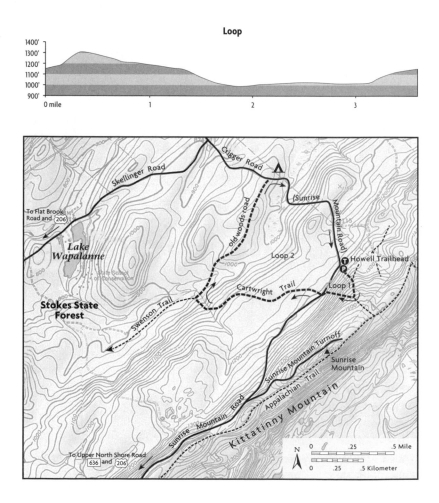

Farley and Lance play swamp hopscotch in the woods.

If you and Bowser are up to some nimble fun, these two short loops will give you both plenty of action. The first loop offers swampy hopscotch and steeplechase-like jumps across downed trees. The second loop makes you feel like no human has gone here before—a real walk in the woods in populated New Jersey, followed by a short uphill walk on the road next to an evergreen forest with a North Woods feel.

The Howell Trail begins as a wide, gravel woods road that heads gently uphill. At 0.25 mile, continue straight on the woods road, although the Howell makes a sharp left turn. This unmarked trail heads up Kittatinny Mountain to the Appalachian Trail. Near the top of a 100-foot climb at about 0.16 mile later, turn right onto an unmarked grassy footpath that leads through open forest. This well-worn path is easy to follow and loops back to Sunrise Mountain Road. Trees of many sizes have fallen across the trail, offering an agility course for your dog. Cross a wet area—great for Bowser to cool off in summer, but be prepared to get your feet wet.

Cross the road and go left for 50 feet, then turn right onto the brown/red-blazed Cartwright Trail. Steep and rocky, the footpath heads steadily downhill, dropping 200 feet through red and white oak and shagbark hickory. In the fall when the leaves cover the twisting path, it can all look the same, so be sure to watch for blazes.

As the trail bends to the right, a stone foundation and a well are evidence of an early 1900s farm. Springs, probably used by the homesteaders, bubble to the surface and flow downhill.

At the bottom of the hill 0.9 mile later, the Cartwright ends at the red-dot Swenson Trail. Turn right onto a fairly level old woods road that soon gets wet and rocky with no immediate blazes. You may wonder where you are, but keep going straight. Soon the road clears and blazes appear. On a gentle climb, pass through mountain laurel and fields of young American beech, oak, and blueberry—prime ursine habitat. Have a nice loud conversation with Bowser. Deer trails disappear into the landscape, and the scenery becomes more floriferous. This level trail ambles through open woods and a 12-acre Forest Management Area, clear-cut to revitalize the forest.

In 1 mile, reach Sunrise Mountain Road again, north of the Howell Trail. Turn right onto the road and enjoy the walk back to the car past tall pines and hemlock, then uphill past a reforestation project and a pond with duck boxes. You can stop at the pond and let Bowser take an on-leash dip to cool off.

A number of trails lead from Sunrise Mountain Road through the forest and up to the ridge to create a hike of any length. Hunting is allowed in the forest, so during the fall hikers should wear blaze orange to be visible. Although Bowser is leashed, he might benefit from a wide orange collar.

3. Paulinskill Valley Trail: Hainesburg to Blairstown

Round-trip: 14.2 miles
Elevation range: 350 feet, flat and steady
Difficulty: Easy
Hiking time: 8 hours
Best canine hiking season: Fall, winter, spring
Regulations: Dogs must be leashed
Maps: USGS Portland, PA quadrangle; Paulinskill Valley Rail-Trail
Information: Kittatinny Valley State Park, (973) 786-6445,
  www.njparksandforests.org, www.pvtc-kvsp.org

Getting there: For a one-way, 7.1-mile hike, take two cars. Take State Route 94 to Blairstown and drop one car at the Foot Bridge Park parking lot, just north of the diner. Drive 6.3 miles south on Route 94 and turn left onto Kill Road in Knowlton. The street sign may be missing, but a large American sycamore stands on the corner. Go over the one-lane bridge and park.

The 26-mile Paulinskill Valley Trail, an abandoned railroad bed converted to state park, offers an easy stroll or fast-paced jog through wild and civilized habitats. When the rocky climbs of nearby mountains are covered in snow, this section beckons the walker and dog through small towns, farms, woods, and an airport, past backyards, and alongside streams and lakes populated with wildlife. History and railroad buffs can enjoy railroad memorabilia, while Fido appreciates the sights and scents of current culture—grazing horses and cows and swimming waterfowl. With plentiful access and parking, it is always close to civilization.

To the right, the grand Hainesburg Viaduct spans the sky as part of the defunct Lackawanna Cutoff that stretched from the Delaware River

The Paulinskill Valley Trail runs under the defunct Hainesburg Viaduct that spans the Delaware River.

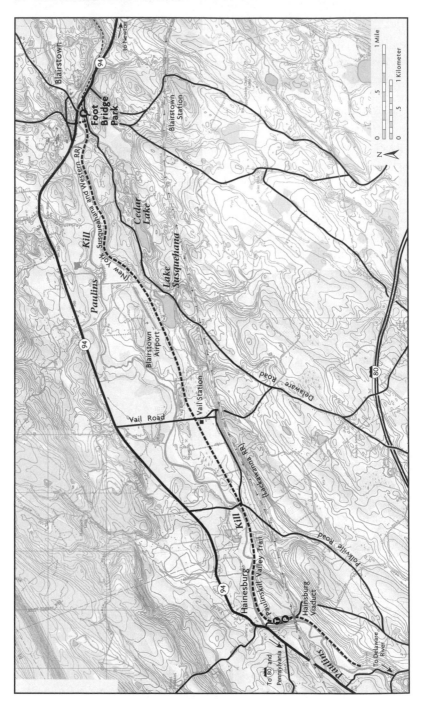

The Paulinskill Valley Trail runs past scenic and historic houses, farms, and fields.

to Port Morris. From here, the trail heads left and north on a strip of roadside grass. The path becomes cinders, a pliable surface that's easy on the legs and paws, like much of the trail. On the left, the Paulins Kill runs fast on its way west to the Delaware River. Mallards, black ducks, Canada and domestic geese, and common mergansers and great blue herons in warm months, abound. Enjoy craggy outcrops and a stream that in spring flows into the Kill from a valley. The river runs beside the trail most of the way, offering numerous cooling-off spots for your dog.

The trail soon runs like a peninsula between the river and the road. Just imagine the defunct New York, Susquehanna, and Western Railroad carrying coal from Pennsylvania and local milk, ice, and wood to New York, chugging through this fertile valley. Pooch likes it too—a quick happy jog for him with the road laid out straight ahead.

From the crossroad at 1.3 miles, it is 1.1 miles to Vail Station through shady maple and red oak woods. A cement railroad mileage marker says "JC 87"—87 miles to the defunct Jersey City terminal. The path slips behind old freight buildings to Vail Road where an eroded cement slab sports a "W"—a whistle stop that signaled the train to sound its whistle at the road crossing. You can turn around and see the Delaware Water Gap from here.

The path skims the edge of the very active Blairstown Airport. Fido may wonder what an airplane is so up close. Keep a tight leash. Turn right at the first taxiway and follow it past Lake Susquehanna and picturesque farm buildings. Cross the road and turn left along the road cut that slices through a cedar-covered hillside and low fields. The Kill and its floodplain appear again, accompanying you and your dog into Blairstown and Foot Bridge Park.

If your dog likes to sniff wildflowers, many bloom alongside the trail under the light canopy in spring. Humans on foot and bicycles, dogs, and horses heavily use this linear, Rails-to-Trails park.

4. Cedar Swamp Trail

Round-trip: 1.5 miles
Elevation range: 1400–1500 feet
Difficulty: Easy
Hiking time: 1 hour
Best canine hiking season: Fall, winter, spring
Regulations: Dogs must be leashed; fee from Memorial Day weekend to Labor Day
Maps: USGS Port Jervis South, NY quadrangle; NJDEP High Point State Park; NY–NJTC Kittatinny Trails Map 18
Information: High Point State Park, (973) 875-4800, *www.njparksandforests.org*

Getting there: Take State Route 23 north past the town of Sussex. Just past the park office on the left, bear right to the gate. Stay on Kuser Road past Lake Marcia, then turn left onto Cedar Swamp Road for 0.6 mile to the trailhead and park.

The Cedar Swamp Trail through the John D. Kuser Natural Area in High Point State Park offers you and your dog an opportunity to

Lance and Little One take the easy way over a glacially carved bog at High Point State Park.

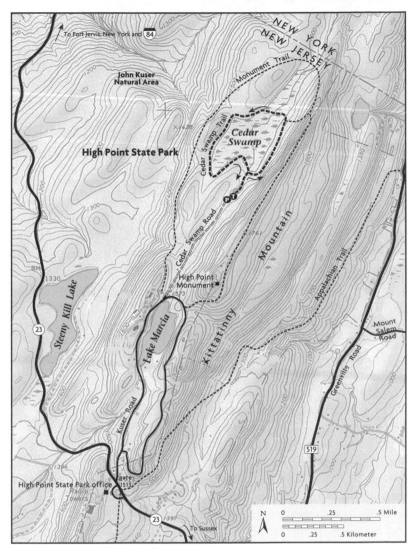

walk on a mountaintop without having to climb the mountain to get there. This is a great hike in winter—fun, fast, and easy. Your dog will enjoy trotting through the different habitats of this ancient lake scoured out of bedrock by the Wisconsin Glacier about twelve thousand years ago. A wide boardwalk traverses part of it, allowing an up-close look at life in a protected bog.

The Cedar Swamp Trail is a lollipop shape enclosed by a larger loop, the Monument Trail. It starts as a gravel road that leads downhill to the

An easy walk through a mountaintop bog on the Cedar Swamp Trail

ancient, 30-acre glacial lake, passing through deciduous woods edged with wildflowers, fragrant sweet ferns, blueberries, and huckleberries. The trail divides at a plaque and the loop begins. Either direction returns to this spot, so you cannot get lost.

To the right, a crushed slate path, quarried at the park, goes through cinnamon fern, massive rhododendron, and hemlock. Your dog will like trotting down this shady path as raucous birdcalls float from the ascending forest on the right. A few trails run off the path, so always bear left, staying close to the bog in the center. One path to the right connects to the Monument Trail for a longer, steeper loop.

A boardwalk seems to float above the peatland and its fascinating plants and creatures. Porcupine, skunk, raccoon, deer, and vole—and if you are lucky, bobcat—residents will keep Fido interested and alert. Watch his ears for a sign that he has scented a forest inhabitant. A walk in each season presents different views—cotton grass and bright berries of mountain holly and arum in fall, blue iris and other bog-loving flowering perennials and frogs in summer, fragrant swamp azalea in spring, and nurseries of sphagnum moss sprouting baby mountain laurel, hemlock, and northern species of spruce year-round. Sedge hummocks support Atlantic white cedar, the dominant tree of the wetter parts.

At the end of the boardwalk, pass black huckleberry, highbush blueberry, and bracken fern as the trail rises above the wetland for a little canine exercise, then dips into an evergreen forest in a carpet of ferns, moss, and lichen-covered rock. In warm weather, this shady area is welcome for human and dog.

The 850-acre swamp is part of the 1451-acre Natural Area, which is preserved under the state's Natural Area System because its habitats support endangered and threatened species such as the Cooper's hawk and three-toothed cinquefoil. Cedar Swamp is at the highest elevation in the world for its type of landform. For a bit more ecology, stop at the office for a brochure.

5. Appalachian Trail: Wantage Foothills

Round-trip: 5.2 miles
Elevation range: 600–700 feet
Difficulty: Easy to lightly moderate
Hiking time: 3 hours
Best canine hiking season: Year-round
Regulations: Dogs must be leashed; carry out dog waste
Maps: USGS Unionville, NY quadrangle, NY-NJTC Appalachian Trail
   Map 4, Hagstrom Morris/Sussex/Warren Counties Atlas
Information: High Point State Park, (973) 875-4800,
   www.njparksandforests.org; www.dec.state.ny.us
   (for NY hunting regulations)

Getting there: From State Route 23 just north of Sussex, turn right onto County Road 651 (Unionville Road), following the sharp bend to the left at 2 miles. Drive another 2.7 miles to Quarry Road on the right. The parking lot is on the left.

For two cars, go to Gemmer Road first. To get there from Route 23 north of Colesville, turn left onto County Route 519 (Mountain Road). Drive 1.3 miles and turn right onto Mount Salem Road. Go about 2 miles and turn left onto Gemmer Road. To drop the other car on Quarry Road, continue on Mount Salem Road for 2.4 miles, turning left onto County Route 651 and immediately right onto Quarry Road.

This short section of the world-famous Appalachian National Scenic Trail (AT) that runs from Georgia to Maine weaves through various habitats, offering your dog the sights and scents of open meadows, shady forest, cool streams, and swampland. A dip in the meandering stream is a treat at the end of the hike.

Cross Quarry Road and head down into the woods toward Georgia. Your dog will smell sweet air in the dappled shade of young woods. Cross

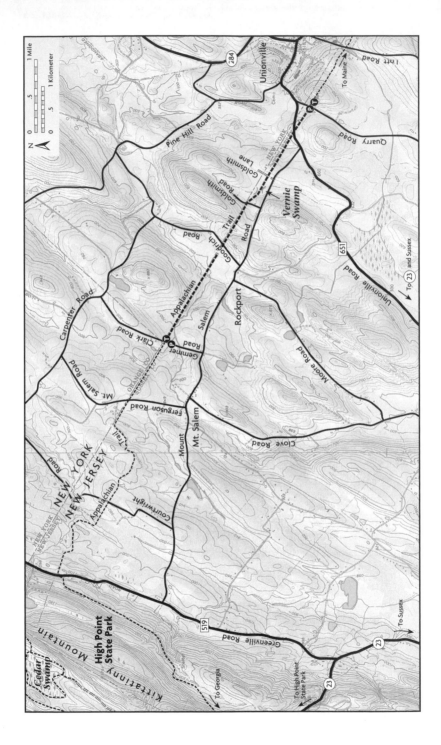

Bob and three generations of ladies pause in the Vernie Swamp.

Unionville Road, go left for 50 feet, then turn right into the woods again. Watch for the white rectangle blazes. The trail crosses many stone walls, reminders of hardy farmers, surrounded by fields of wildflowers and blackberries in summer. The path is soft dirt with few rocks, unlike the trail farther west on the Kittatinny Ridge.

A few short, steep uphills through open woods are capped with shade, just waiting for your dog. Cross the dirt Goldsmith Lane at 0.7 mile. The path goes down to Vernie Swamp. A raised boardwalk spans this often flooded, prehistoric-looking wetland. Your dog will enjoy the cooler air and different scents. A lower boardwalk covers a portion of the trail that gets wet and muddy, although Bowser may prefer to walk in the mud. Winter is a great time to hike here. With temperatures in the thirties, the mud freezes but you and your dog stay warm by hiking.

The trail rises to a wide rock slab and turns sharply left along the rock. Cross the gravel Goldsmith Road into woods at 1.1 miles, then continue up through sunny hillside fields with a great view of the High Point Monument and back into shade. The trail edges a concrete dam and pond, traveling within 50 feet of the New York border. Check the websites for both states for hunting dates in New Jersey and Westtown, New York.

At 1.6 miles, cross Goodrich Road and follow the stream for a mile with many spots for Spot to get his belly wet. Wooden bridges cross the stream to hike's end, or turn around at Gemmer Road. Your dog will find this hike short and interesting.

6. Spring Lake Loop

Round-trip: 2.8 miles
Elevation range: 500–560 feet
Difficulty: Easy
Hiking time: 1.5 hours
Best canine hiking season: Year-round
Regulations: Dogs must be leashed
Maps: USGS Newton West, NJ quadrangle, NJDEP Swartswood
State Park
Information: Swartswood State Park, (973) 383-5230,
www.njparksandforests.org

Getting there: From US Highway 206 in Newton, take County Route 519 North. Go 0.3 mile and turn left at the light onto County Route

The Spring Lake Trail rises through cool hemlock woods.

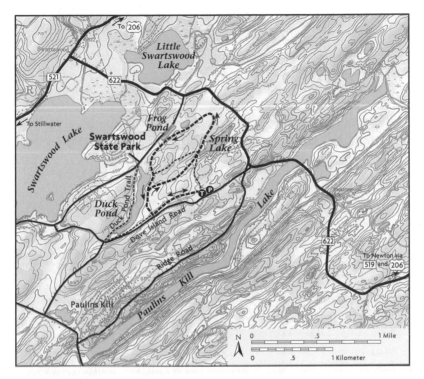

622 West (Swartswood Road). Drive 3.4 miles and turn left at the top of a hill onto Ridge Road. Turn right immediately onto Dove Island Road. The equestrian parking lot is 0.5 mile on the right.

This path through mostly lowland offers man and best friend an easy hike in the Great Limestone Valley that follows the southern edge of the Appalachian Mountains. The white-blazed Spring Lake Trail is open to equestrians, so most paths are wide. Your dog will like the quiet with just the sounds of birdsong and scampering chipmunks and squirrels. The paths are smooth and the hills are gentle.

Enter the woods on an unblazed trail and bear left at the T intersection onto a mowed equestrian path through shady forest. Remember this spot at the big white ash tree for when you return. You will soon pick up a blaze. Where the white-blazed equestrian trail goes left to connect to the paved Duck Pond Trail, bear right onto the footpath.

Go right on the green-blazed trail that connects you to the white again near Spring Lake. Cross a stone wall on the downhill and, at another T where the green meets the white trail, go left. See Spring Lake ahead of you through the trees, or take a few minutes for a jaunt to the lake.

The trail heads left, uphill, leaving the lake on your right. Pass Frog Pond, a vernal pond that dries in summer, and hike under cool hemlock woods. The trail passes over a number of stone walls built by farmers long ago.

Soon Duck Pond appears on the right. Watch for the unmarked narrow path that brings you back to the parking lot. The white trail bears left there, but you go straight.

Blue and green trails connect parts of the white trail loop for a slightly longer hike.

7. Karamac–Dunnfield Creek Loop

Round-trip: 5 miles, plus 0.5 mile to and from trails
Elevation range: 300–1000 feet
Difficulty: Moderate
Hiking time: 3.5 hours
Best canine hiking season: Year-round
Regulations: Dogs must be leashed
Maps: USGS Portland, PA quadrangle; NY-NJTC Kittatinny Trails
    Map 15; NJDEP Worthington State Forest; Delaware Water Gap
    National Recreation Area
Information: Worthington State Forest, (908) 841-9575,
    www.njparksandforests.org

Getting there: From Interstate 80 West, take exit 1, the last exit in New Jersey before the Delaware River Toll Bridge into Pennsylvania. Go left under Route 80 and park at the National Park Service Visitor Center by the river. Walk north between Route 80 and the river.

This trail has the best of both worlds for you and your dog—solitude in quiet, almost undisturbed nature on one side of the Kittatinny Ridge

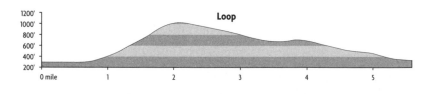

Field of ferns on the Beaulahland Trail in Worthington State Forest

and a popular glacial stream on the other. A short jaunt across the Appalachian Trail connects both sides of the mountain.

Cross under the highway at the three-minute traffic light on Old Mine Road. An iron pole heralds the trailhead of the Karamac Trail, an old railbed, on the left. Take this footpath along the river past vestiges of metal bodies and the ruins of a railroad bridge that once spanned this swift river. Your dog will enjoy the sights and sounds of river life. At 1 mile, the trail turns landward, rising 200 feet past scant ruins of a hotel, crosses Old Mine Road, and ends in the Farview parking lot at 1.2 mile.

Take the yellow-blazed Beulahland Trail (Farview Trail on some maps) uphill on a woods road through a landscape of ferns. At 1.4 miles, reach a ridge-top junction of the white-blazed Appalachian Trail. Cross it onto the red-blazed Holly Springs Trail into cathedral-like woods. Head

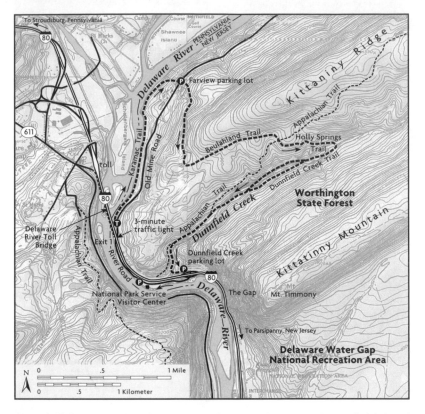

downhill for 0.5 mile, then turn right onto the green Dunnfield Creek Trail. But first, stop, look, and listen for the water. Give Pooch a drink while you look around and enjoy these gorgeous woods. There is sanctity about them. Pooch will most likely know he is in a place much out of the ordinary.

Descend for 2 miles through a hemlock ravine with a creek full of boulders and lined in ferns and rhododendron. The boulders are a natural agility course for your dog, who will enjoy picking his way across this interesting terrain. The creek has little waterfalls and pools of almost-still water. The trail rambles around the creek, crossing it frequently on bridges and boulders with a 600-foot descent to the parking lot. There, turn left alongside Route 80 and follow the road under the highway back to the visitor center.

During the summer and on weekends, the Dunnfield side of the mountain is a popular place to be, with good reason. Keep a good grip on your dog on this very fun hike.

8. Pochuck Boardwalk

Round-trip: 2 miles
Elevation range: 420 feet, flat and steady
Difficulty: Easy
Hiking time: 1.5 hours
Best canine hiking season: Year-round
Regulations: Dogs must be leashed; carry out waste
Maps: USGS Wawayanda, NJ quadrangle; NY-NJTC Appalachian
   Trail Map 4
Information: Wawayanda State Park, (973) 853-4462,
   www.njparksandforests.org

Getting there: Take State Route 94 to McAfee and turn right onto County Route 517 North. Drive 6.3 miles to a natural area with a boardwalk on the right. Park along the right side of the road, just before Carol Drive and a development.

Turtles sun on a log in Pochuck Creek floodplain—a common sight from the boardwalk.

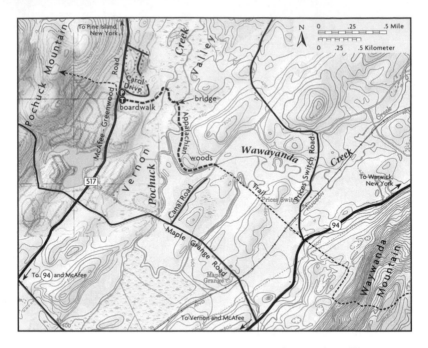

On this short section of the Appalachian Trail between Pochuck and Wawayanda Mountains in the Vernon Valley, you and your dog can immerse yourselves in the life of a freshwater marsh without getting wet. From the safety of a mile-long, sunny boardwalk, you both can see and sniff marsh critters like turtles and water snakes and a plethora of wild flowers and cattails. The trail offers an expansive view of the valley.

The boardwalk traverses the 3000-foot-wide floodplain of 60-foot-wide (at times) Pochuck Creek. The National Park Service classifies the floodplain as an "Exceptional Resource Value Wetland" with its tributaries and quagmire. When the creek floods, so does the floodplain, forming an image of the ancient glacial lake it once was. A 110-foot-long wooden suspension bridge crosses the stream, providing a different experience for hiker and dog.

Put on insect lotion, and a hankie with eucalyptus oil on Bowser, and set off across the boardwalk, zigzagging through cattails. Sniff the fragrance of flowers and listen to cicadas. Early morning, especially, presents a bit of the extra fun of bird- and raptor-watching. Benches along the way provide great spots for contemplation for you and your dog.

Cross the bridge and take Bowser down to the water for a good soaking in warm weather. Continue on to where the boardwalk ends at the woods—good for a quick, shady exploration. Turn around and go back the same way. You will never get lost on this hike.

This is the perfect place for you and your dog to get some much-needed winter exercise. Many feet and paws pack down the snow, and you and Bowser can easily see the tracks of the floodplains' wild inhabitants. The boardwalk is popular with groups of school kids who come out to learn about nature.

9. Sussex Branch: Warbasse Junction to Augusta Hill Road

Round-trip: 8.6 miles

Elevation range: 500–560 feet

Difficulty: Easy

Hiking time: 4 hours

Best canine hiking season: Year-round

Regulations: Dogs must be leashed; carry out dog waste

Maps: USGS Newton East, NJ quadrangle, Paulinskill Valley Rail-Trail

Information: Kittatinny Valley State Park, (973) 786-6445, *www.pvtc-kvsp.org; www.njparksandforests.org*

Getting there: Take State Route 15 North to Lafayette. Turn left onto State Route 94 South at the traffic light. Drive 0.8 mile and turn left onto Warbasse Junction Road (County Route 663 South). Drive 0.5 mile to the parking lot on the right. With two cars, take Route 15 North to US Highway 206 North. Drive 1 mile and turn left onto Augusta Hill Road at the traffic light, and park at 0.1 mile on the right.

This section of the 20-mile Sussex Branch Trail follows the Paulins Kill, offering your dog several opportunities for a drink and a swim at each bridge crossing. This well-maintained, popular path is cool and easy on Fido's feet.

From the southern trailhead, walk across County Route 663 and take the Paulinskill Valley Trail for 225 feet to the trail junction in the woods. This is Warbasse Junction, an old-time crossroads of two defunct railroad beds, now the Sussex Branch Trail and Paulinskill Valley Trail. Turn left onto the Sussex Branch. There is no sign here, just a wooden bench. Cross over the Kill on a wide bridge—the first of six on this hike—where Fido can take a dip in the stream.

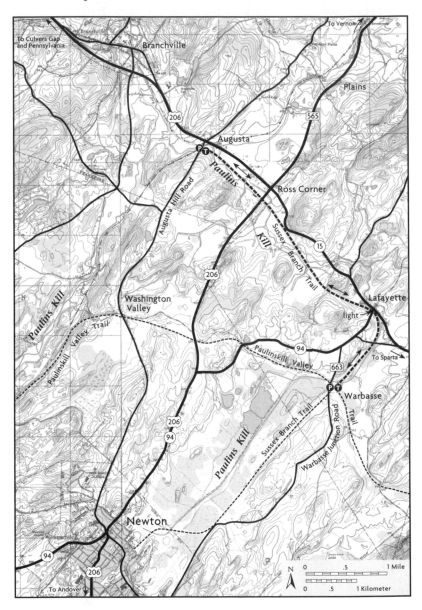

Paulins Kill, edged in wildflowers, flows under the trail six times.

After crossing State Route 94 at 0.8 mile, the Kill comes close to your right, so it is easy to amble down the short bank to the stream. Cross country roads and then Route 206 at 3.3 miles.

The trail is mostly sunny with dappled shade, and the Kill weaves back and forth across it. In spots, the trail remains moist and cool for Fido's feet. Edging the deciduous woods, wildflowers abound in the sun.

10. Buttermilk Falls Loop

Round-trip: 5 miles
Elevation range: 500–1600 feet
Difficulty: Difficult
Hiking time: 4.5 hours
Best canine hiking season: Spring, summer, fall
Regulations: Dogs must be on a 6-foot leash
Maps: USGS Lake Maskenozha, PA and Flatbrookville, Newton West, and Culvers Gap, NJ quadrangles; NY-NJTC North Kittatinny Trails Map 17
Information: Delaware Water Gap National Recreation Area headquarters, (570) 588-2435, and visitor center, (908) 496-4458, *www.nps.gov/dewa*

Watching the water fall 204 feet at Buttermilk Falls—a good spot for a doggy dunk

Getting there: Take US Highway 206 North. Turn left onto Struble Road (Dimon Road) in Sandyston (just past the Stokes State Forest office) for 3.8 miles. Turn right onto Tillman Road for 0.9 mile (Brink Road, a dirt road, is on the left), then go left onto Mountain Road, a rutted, gravel road with a lot of wildflowers, for 1.9 miles to the parking lot on the right. In winter, Mountain Road is not maintained and drivers must drive at their own risk.

This hike offers as close to a wilderness experience as possible for Fido and companion in New Jersey, for few people climb beyond the falls and this section of the Appalachian Trail (AT) is far from any crossroad. Fido will enjoy the falls, woods, meadows, ridge-top breeze, and the cooling walk back on the moist Woods Trail. In spring and after heavy rains, the 204-foot Buttermilk Falls is spectacular. This rugged trail is for dogs and people with hiking experience only. Carry at least 3 liters of drinking water for Fido and 3 liters for you.

The blue-blazed Buttermilk Falls Trail starts at the falls where Fido may want to wade in the shallow pool at the bottom. Climb the steep stairs, some with open risers, along the falls under hemlock, mountain laurel, and rhododendron that bloom in June.

Cross the stream on a bridge—the last of civilization Fido will see for a while—then head uphill to the right following the blue trail. At about 0.5 mile, the trail emerges onto a mountainside meadow with wildflowers. Buttermilk Falls Brook cascades down through the ravine to the left. Cross the Woods Trail, an old woods road, at 1100 feet. Continuing uphill, walk along an exposed rock face, open with cool breezes.

At a T junction at about 1.3 miles at 1600 feet, turn left onto the AT, here an old gravel road once part of a development plan. A wooden sign says it is 2 miles back down the blue trail to the bottom of Buttermilk Falls. This is actual mileage, taking in the vertical climbs and downhills, rather than a horizontal map reading.

The AT's white rectangular blazes soon appear on this path that ambles through sun and woods and over outcrops. Fido will enjoy exploring

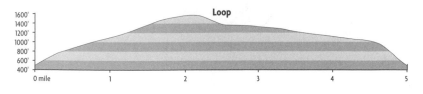

and sniffing the trail's many habitats, and you can enjoy ripe blueberries in July.

About 1 mile later, the trail dips 200 feet with a campsite on the right. Go about 20 feet to a faint T intersection. The AT goes off to the right but, instead, make a quick left onto an obvious unmarked path, the first noticeable trail since Buttermilk Falls.

Moss covers the path, cool for Fido's feet. Just after the wetland on the right, turn left onto the forested Woods Trail and head back to the blue, paralleling the AT. In about 0.5 mile, the road rejoins the blue Buttermilk Falls Trail with a "WOODS TRAIL" sign tacked to a birch on the left. Turn right and head downhill on the same trail through meadow and woods to the brook that feeds the falls—a welcoming spot for Fido to take a dip.

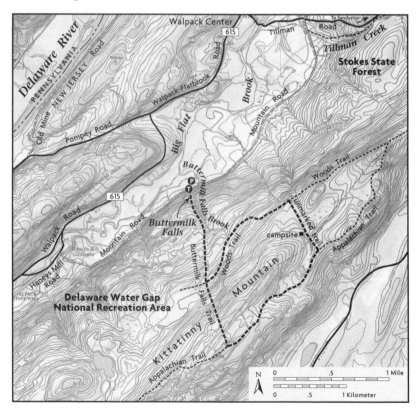

11. Tillman Ravine

Round-trip: 2 miles
Elevation range: 450–820 feet
Difficulty: Easy
Hiking time: 1.5 hours (longer for added walk to river)
Best canine hiking season: Spring, summer, fall
Regulations: Dogs must be leashed
Maps: USGS Culvers Gap, NJ quadrangle; NY-NJTC Kittatinny Trails
Map 17; NJDEP Stokes State Forest
Information: Stokes State Forest, (973) 948-3820,
www.njparksandforests.org; Delaware Water Gap National
Recreation Area headquarters, (570) 588-2435, and visitor center,
(908) 496-4458, *www.nps.gov/dewa*

Getting there: Take US Highway 206 North. Turn left onto Struble Road
(Dimon Road) in Sandyston—just past the Stokes State Forest headquarters on the right. Drive 3.8 miles through forest with red pine plantations
planted by the Civilian Conservation Corps in the 1930s. Turn right onto
Tillman Road. Parking lot is 0.3 mile on the left.

Tillman Ravine is an easy hike through tall evergreens that evoke Hansel
and Gretel's wooded path. Bowser will enjoy the forest's primeval quality. Here, the Tillman Brook slices through the northwestern slope of
Kittatinny Mountain, creating a dramatic gorge with a racing stream,
waterfalls, and eddies—places for you and your dog to chill on a hot day.
Masses of rhododendron bloom in early summer. Tillman Ravine is a 525-
acre, state-designated Natural Area because of its geological significance
and mature hemlock-mixed hardwood forest.

Follow the red-triangle-blazed trail to the left under red pine and hemlock, following the sound of the brook. Tillman Brook begins 0.5 mile
north of the gorge, and spring seeps feed it on its way to Big Flat Brook.
At about 0.25 mile, the trail splits off to the right, but you stay along the

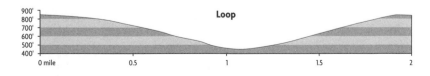

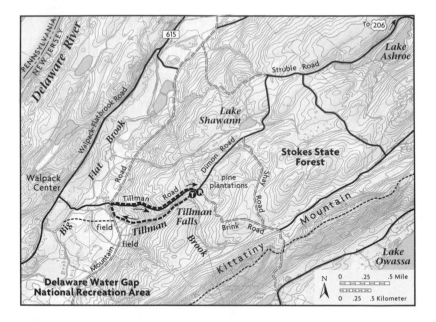

water. A maze of short trails rambles through this part of the ravine, but you can't get lost in this area bounded by the brook and roads.

Bowser will enjoy the variety of terrain as the trail rises and falls in short bursts, crosses the stream on wooden bridges, steps over uplifted rock, and climbs stone stairs carved from bedrock and others formed by oak and hemlock roots. The stream's "teacups," bowl-shaped potholes formed by swirling sand in fast-moving runoff, are inviting in the heat of summer. The spray of the stream cools the air, and fragrance from trees including autumn olive and American basswood scent the walk in spring.

Chunks of exposed bedrock—red-, green-, and olive-colored sandstone—display folds and fractures along the brook. As the stream's energy levels off, so do the trail and landscape, and artifacts from prior human use appear downstream. The water is deeper and quieter. Just before a cement-covered stone dam wrecked upon the far shore, cross the stream on rocks and patches of ground (a good hiking stick helps here) and check out the field, farmed in the 1970s, beyond a stone wall. Bowser can easily wade across the cool water.

The ravine ends at Mountain Road. Turn right and right again onto Tillman Road, with an ancient cemetery on the left. A variety of wildflowers grow along the uphill road back to the parking lot. Or, for a longer

*Tillman Brook is strewn with moss-covered boulders and decorated with
July-blooming rhododendron.*

walk, follow the stream out to Mountain Road and turn left, then quickly right for 0.3 mile through fields, along a tree line and through woods to Big Flat Brook, a fast-moving stream and Tillman Brook's end, where you and your dog can take a real dip. This is National Recreation Area land, and Fido must be on a leash.

To get back to the car from the field, turn left onto the dirt road (Mountain Road) and pick up the trail again just after the cement bridge on the right, or walk to the crossroad and turn right to walk up the macadam road under a cool canopy of hemlock, white pine, oak, and hickory.

12. Appalachian Trail: Vernon Valley

One-way: 14.4 miles
Elevation range: 400–1080 feet
Difficulty: Moderate to difficult
Hiking time: 2 days
Best canine hiking season: June through September
Regulations: Dogs must be on a 6-foot leash
Maps: USGS Hamburg and Wawayanda, NJ and Unionville, NY
   quadrangles; NY-NJTC Appalachian Trail Map 4
Information: High Point State Park, (973) 875-4800, Wawayanda
   State Park, (973) 853-4462, *www.njparksandforests.org*

Getting there: Take two cars, or have someone drop you off in Sussex and leave your car in Vernon. If you are taking two cars, drop the first one off at the Appalachian Trail (AT) parking lot in Vernon and the second one on Goldsmith Lane in Sussex. From State Route 23 in Hamburg, take State Route 94 North through Vernon for 7.8 miles and turn right into the parking lot (0.6 mile after Maple Grange Road). To get to Goldsmith Lane, take Route 23 North to north of Sussex and turn right onto County Route 651 (Unionville Road) for 4 miles. Turn left onto Mount Salem

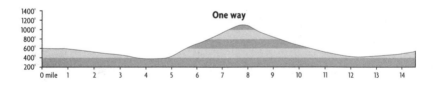

A mountaintop is the place to be to catch a wonderful breeze and a great view.

Road, then right onto the dirt Goldsmith Lane and park off the road. Put a sign in your car window giving your expected hiking route to let people know where you are and why your car is there.

This section of the Appalachian National Scenic Trail is relatively easy and a joy to hike, with great views through the Kittatinny Valley along the New York–New Jersey border. Traverse bucolic farmland, wild-flower meadows, railroad beds, streams, a wildlife refuge, and Pochuck Mountain.

Day 1 (7 miles): From Goldsmith Lane, head east into the woods on a soft path edged with club moss. The rock-free trail crosses County Route 651 and Quarry Road, then climbs a small hill through stands of spring-blooming shadbush scattered with remnants of homesteads and a field of wildflowers.

The trail comes out at Lott Road where a creek runs under it. A stone wall edges the woods—a great place to take off your pack and refresh Bowser before the climb into the woods. Cross the wooden bridge and head upslope along a hillside with large black cherry trees. The cin-dered path is an abandoned railroad bed with a cement mile marker that says "JC73"—73 miles to the terminal at Jersey City. New Jersey's woods are loaded with history. Cross State Route 284 into woods and farms with mown paths through meadows, then around a hay field to Oil City Road.

Hike a short, steep climb to a meadow at 607 feet overlooking the Wallkill River National Wildlife Refuge with Pochuck Mountain across the valley in the distance. Walk through wildflowers, then descend into young woods. Turn left onto small Carnegie Road, then right onto Oil City Road again, a country road here with no sense of civilization except for two old houses and a small stone barn.

Cross the bridge over the Wallkill River and stop under the shade trees with tall benches, just the right height for removing your pack and putting it on again easily. Your dog can take a dip in the river to get cool—on leash, of course. Continue down the road and turn right into the wildlife refuge and onto the joint AT/Liberty Loop Trail that surrounds impoundments managed for waterfowl. Dogs must be leashed and are only allowed on the AT in the refuge. The trail enters the woods on boards over a wet area. Bring mosquito juice!

Cross Wallkill-Liberty Corners Road and take the soft path up the hill onto Pochuck Mountain. Your dog will enjoy climbing Pochuck Mountain with its roundabout ups and downs. At about 0.1 mile up, look for a sign for water to the left. The NJDEP bought this house for the well, and good water is available to hikers from a spigot out back, except in winter when the pipes are drained. Look out over the valley you just hiked, back to the High Point Monument on the Kittatinny Ridge. Set up camp about 0.5 mile from the house at the Pochuck Mountain Shelter, complete with bear box, privy, picnic table, and flat tent sites.

Day 2 (7.4 miles): Pochuck Mountain is a mini mountain range unto itself. This section has a steep rock scramble that rewards you and your canine pal with views to the Kittatinny Ridge and Shawangunks in New York. Other things to notice include ravines with rhododendron that bloom in July, lichen-covered bedrock, a grassy hillock with views, and maybe a baby bear climbing a tree—but if you see one, watch for mama. Your dog will enjoy the varying terrain and habitats.

Near the bottom, there's "trail magic" in a box near a water sign, and a trail register offers kudos to the "trail angels" who supply this unexpected kindness. Trail angels are individuals, in this case a married couple, who, acting on their own for a myriad of heartfelt reasons, regularly bring food, magazines, water, and health-care products to shelters for AT thru-hikers, and sometimes hikers are lucky enough to meet one in person and be taken to a local restaurant for a real treat or to a store to replenish their supplies.

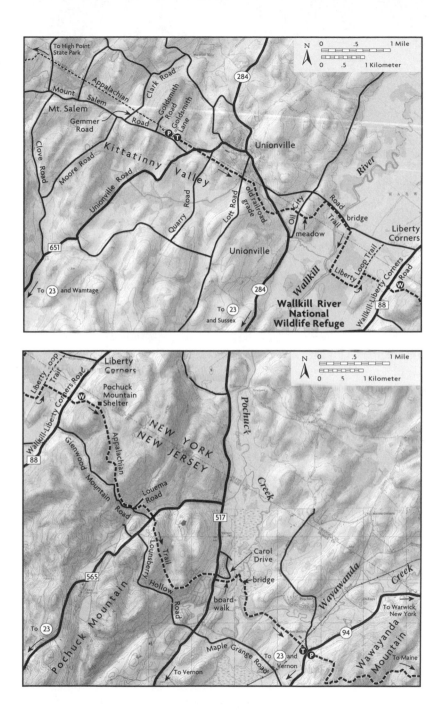

Petey is the last to rise and shine at Pochuck shelter.

The trail crosses private, gravel Louema Road into woods. Cross County Route 565 2.8 miles from the shelter, still on the downslope to County Route 517.

The AT boardwalk zigzags above swamp and wildflowers and crosses the Pochuck Quagmire Suspension Bridge built by New York–New Jersey Trail Conference volunteers and Wawayanda State Park staff. Pochuck Creek is a good spot for your dog to cool his paws after the sunny boardwalk. The path enters a forest of shagbark hickory with stone walls and cool ground. Evidence of old farmsteads lurks. The trail briefly follows a bike path, crosses Wawayanda Creek, continues through old fields and young woods with ancient fruit trees and once-planted roses framing glimpses of farm fields. Toward Wawayanda Mountain, the trail passes open woods, stone walls, wild turkeys, a railroad crossing, and a stile on the way to the parking lot on Route 94.

13. Appalachian Trail: Culvers Lake to Buttermilk Falls

One-way: 10.5 miles
Elevation range: 500–1600 feet
Difficulty: Moderate with steep descent
Hiking time: 2 days
Best canine hiking season: June through September
Regulations: Dogs must be on a 6-foot leash

Maps: USGS Lake Maskenozha, PA and Flatbrookville, Newton West, and Culvers Gap, NJ quadrangles; NY-NJTC Kittatinny Trails Map 17; NJDEP Stokes State Forest

Information: Delaware Water Gap National Recreation Area, (570) 828-2253, *www.nps.gov/dewa;* Stokes State Forest, (973) 948-3820, *www.njparksandforests.org*

Getting there: Take two cars, dropping the first car off at Buttermilk Falls. To get to Buttermilk Falls, take US Highway 206 North to north of Branchville. Turn left onto Struble Road (Dimon Road) in Sandyston, just north of the Stokes State Forest office, for 3.8 miles. Turn right onto Tillman Road for 0.9 mile (Brink Road, a dirt road, is on the left) to the stop sign at Walpack Cemetery. Turn left onto Mountain Road, a rutted, gravel road that travels through a lot of wildflowers, for 1.9 miles to the parking lot on the right.

Drop the second car at Stokes State Forest. Stop in at the office and pick up a free overnight parking permit for the Culvers Gap parking lot. Back on Route 206 South, turn left onto Upper North Shore Road. Make an immediate left onto Sunrise Mountain Road and another left into the parking lot. Walk out and cross Route 206, heading south. The trail is to the left along a guardrail.

This section of the 2160 mile Appalachian National Scenic Trail (AT) follows the ridge of Kittatinny Mountain. As in most of New Jersey, the trail is rocky with a lot of ups and downs, but "the climbs are worth the views," said one thru-hiker on her way to Maine. Novice humans and energetic canines will find this to be a leisurely, fun hike, like going on vacation, if done at a comfortable pace over two days. Start early enough to take your time and arrive at the AT shelter well before nightfall. Hikers can sleep in the shelter that thru-hikers share, so be sure to keep your dog on a leash at all times, even when sleeping. Space is on a first-come, first-served basis, so bring your tent to pitch if necessary or if you prefer. Be sure to carry enough water for you and your dog for the day, and bring a water purification kit.

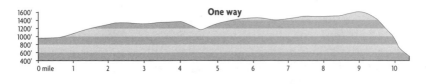

Damien, John, and Chloe hike the Kittatinny Ridge near Brinks Road.

With a stream for fresh water, depending on rainfall, an open-air privy for a fun outdoor experience, a bear box to put your and Fido's food in, short hikes, and awesome views of the Garden State, this overnight hike is a perfect way to get your dog's paws wet. She will enjoy an array of scents while trotting over varied terrain—outcrops, streams, grassy paths, meadows, waterfalls, and woods. You will both meet a lot of day hikers and thru-hikers, many with dogs, on this popular stretch of the AT.

Day 1 (4.5 miles): The narrow, slanted, rocky path with white-rectangle blazes heads up into the forest. Ferns cover the ground. Cross a powerline and a woods road, and hike along the edge of a steep hillside. Keep a tight leash on your dog here among the boulders and shale, and keep his nose out of holes. This south-facing hillside seems like good snake habitat. If you doubt where the trail is, notice cairns in a zigzag pattern and follow them.

Once on top of the ridge and hiking on grass and rock outcrops at over 1300 feet, look back to your left for a great view of Culvers Lake and the Kittatinny Valley. After 2 miles, pass the blue/grey-dot blaze for the Jacobs Ladder Trail. Delicious blueberries and regenerating white pine abound as the trail dips slightly through close vegetation and rises onto grassy outcrops—have a loud conversation as you pass through vegetation, for this is prime bear habitat. Pass a creatures' watering hole, then scale rock slabs long ago tossed on their sides.

At 4.3 miles, turn right onto Brink Road, a forest road. Arrive at Brink Shelter in 0.2 mile on the right. Scout out the camp's accoutrements in daylight.

Day 2 (6 miles): Turn left onto the forest road, and 0.2 mile later, turn right onto the AT at a wooden sign and white blaze. The climb takes you

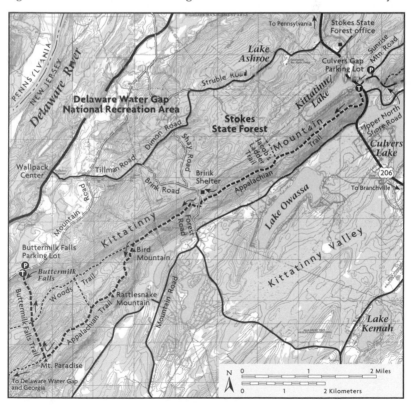

Buttermilk Falls

to Bird Mountain at 1497 feet with wide views to the northwest over the Delaware Valley to Pennsylvania. Now in the Delaware Water Gap National Recreation Area, the walk is fairly level to Rattlesnake Mountain. Watch for blazes on outcrops.

The trail undulates through groves of black birch, mountain laurel, and across water, to the next peak of scrub oak and pitch pine. Take short spurs to the ridge's edge for unforgettable views. Notice skinny deer trails toward the edges. Descend over a footbridge into a hemlock–mountain laurel ravine, then climb steeply for a short bit.

The path gets wide and gravelly. Years ago, plans were made to build houses and roads on this ridge top. At a wooden sign and blue blazes, turn right onto the blue-dot Buttermilk Falls Trail for the 2-mile downhill trek. Due to reblazing, both light blue rectangles and dark blue dots lead to the same place, downhill to the falls.

Hike with care on autumn's leaves through hemlock, moss, and rock. About halfway, cross the Woods Trail, an old forest road, then hike alongside the edge of a ravine. In this habitat of botanical drama where gypsy moths have left their mark on leafless oaks, wildflowers take advantage and grow in the sun and silky sedges edge the cliff. Tack slowly down through steep woods to the Buttermilk stream and follow it to the 204-foot falls, spectacular in spring and after a good rain.

THE HIGHLANDS

Some of the rock in the Highlands is more than a billion years old. This oldest rock in New Jersey was formed during the Precambrian Era, practically off the geologic time charts. The rock forming these ancient mountains came from lava flows and volcanoes, and sediments were deposited when the Proto-Atlantic Ocean covered the land about 500 million years ago. Over time, the rock underwent intense heat and pressure, turning it into harder metamorphic rock.

Glaciers scraped across the Highlands to form the state's three largest lakes—Lake Hopatcong, Budd Lake, and Greenwood Lake—and altered its landforms much as in the Ridge and Valley, but with broader ridges, steeper hillsides, and narrower valleys. In winter, the valleys shelter hikers from wind.

It is a flashy landscape with great exposed piles of melted-looking purple puddingstone, fabulous views of northern New Jersey and New York, spanking clean ridge tops covered in winter green, rushing streams, swamps, sheer rock walls, extinct iron mines and furnaces, and half of New Jersey's water supply. These assets contribute to dramatic hikes for you and your dog, with a lot of twists and turns and unexpected fun.

As part of the New England Uplands, the Highlands spread southwest to northeast from Pennsylvania's Reading Prong to Vermont's Green Mountains.

Two long-distance trails traverse the Highlands—the teal-diamond-blazed Highlands Trail and the white-blazed Patriots Path. The Highlands Trail rambles over preexisting and new trails and roads. When completed, it will extend 160 miles from Storm King in New York to Phillipsburg on the Delaware River. At this writing, about 130 miles are blazed, with remaining sections to be completed mostly in Hunterdon County and a few in Sussex and Morris Counties. For updates, check the New York–New Jersey Trail Conference website at *www.nynjtc.org*.

Patriots Path is a 50-mile trail-network-in-progress linking all types of open spaces. It runs beside three rivers, over mountains, and along pavement. For updates, check *www.parks.morris.nj.us*. All over the Highlands, lands managed by federal, state, county, and municipal entities offer abundant opportunities for you and Fido to hike.

14. Old Guard Trail

Round-trip: 6 miles
Elevation range: 600–1100 feet
Difficulty: Moderately difficult
Hiking time: 6 hours
Best canine hiking season: Fall, winter, spring
Regulations: Dogs must be leashed
Maps: USGS Ramsey, NJ quadrangle; NY-NJTC North Jersey Trails
    Map 115; Ramapo Valley Reservation Camp Glen Gray
Information: Ramapo Valley County Reservation, (201) 327-3500;
    Bergen County Department of Parks and Recreation, (201) 336-7275
    www.co.bergen.nj.us/Parks/Contact.htm

Getting there: Take Interstate 287 to exit 57 onto Skyline Drive and park at milepost 1.4, on the left. The trailhead for the orange-blazed Schuber Trail is across the road at the Camp Tamarack sign.

This rugged hike in Camp Glen Gray in Mahwah has a lot of inducements for a visit by you and your dog in every season. Winter is special in these quiet woods, when bare trees afford great views on the ridges. The mountains provide protection from wind, and continuous ups and downs over the assemblage of hills in the Ramapo Mountains make this hike an aerobic adventure that will keep both you and your dog plenty warm. Expect a lot of camping groups in the summer, although wildflowers, such as prickly pear and pale corydalis tucked among outcrops, are a delight to see then.

The footpath follows rolling terrain through young deciduous woods, outcrops with ledges, and a couple of streams to cross where your dog can

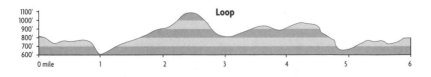

Hikers take a detour to see Lake Vreeland's dam at Camp Glen Gray.
The trail goes over the causeway.

get cool. The trail turns left onto an old woods road by Lake Vreeland and heads uphill past camp cabins where there is usually activity. Somehow the trail is always in a valley except for when reaching the ridge tops. At 1.2 miles from the trailhead, the Schuber Trail joins the Old Guard Trail, blazed with a green tulip tree leaf on white metal, just across a wooden bridge over North Brook, which feeds the lake.

Turn left onto the Old Guard Trail as it trundles uphill on the original Cannonball Road, past a wooden shed on the left that houses a useable well to fill up water bottles that you and your canine pal will appreciate later. Soon bear left into the woods on a footpath that parallels the brook. Small springs trickle year-round from this rocky land and remain unfrozen. At 1.4 miles, as the Schuber departs to the right, bear left and follow the Old Guard over a tributary on stable rocks, then continue under red, white, and chestnut oak, American beech, maple, birch, and patches of mountain laurel. Almost a cross-country agility course, the path traverses a lot of quick ups and downs, skirting rock ledges and wetland. This trail is so new that lowbush blueberries and grasses still cover the unworn path. Walkers must be vigilant about watching for blazes. A 2-foot cut in a downed tree in "gateway" fashion is also a good indication of the trail.

Cross the Algonquin Gas Transmission Company pipeline at 1.9 miles,

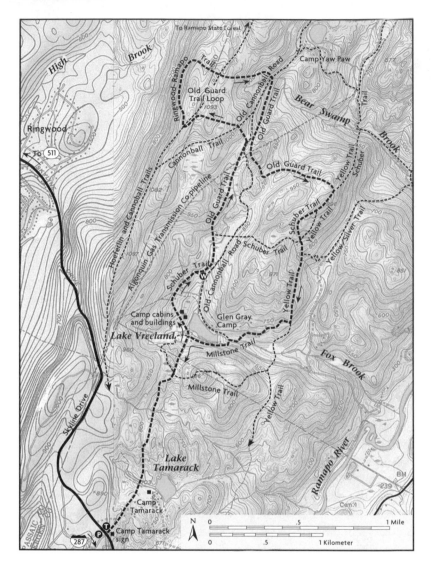

where the path briefly joins the Cannonball Trail, red-blazed with a white C, then bears left into the woods of the camp's North Quad. Sidle along a fun ledge to walk with a valley dropping off sharply to the right—a good place to keep a tight rein on spunky Spike. The path follows the edge of the mountain for views across a valley when the trees are leafless, then reaches the 1100-foot ridge top at 2.3 miles.

Cross the yellow-blazed Hoeferlin Trail at 2.5 miles. Along the chestnut oak–covered ridge, glimpse blue mountains until the trail slips down into woods and eventually encounters a rock shelter—a good spot to take a break from the windy ridge and let Spike have a drink and a snack—then heads up again to join the red-blazed Ringwood-Ramapo Trail to an outcrop with great views of the Wanaque Reservoir and the Wyanokie Mountains westward, Sterling Forest to the northwest, and Erskine Lake in the foreground. Stay on the Old Guard as it bears right toward the east and leaves the red trail, which goes north into Ramapo State Forest. Cross the yellow trail again and, at 3.1 miles, the red-blazed Cannonball that now runs on the original Cannonball Road that was used to carry heavy equipment through the mountains during the Revolutionary War.

After a rocky uphill where you and your dog will get a quick workout, cross the pipeline again. Here you have choices. To cut a mile off the planned hike, turn right, walk 150 yards on the pipeline, and turn left into the woods to head back the way you came.

Or, instead, take the trail ahead of you over rocky climbs, descents, and streams. Just past two iron mine pits on the right, the trail ends on a ridge at 4.1 miles, where it meets the Schuber Trail again and also the yellow-blazed Yellow Trail. Walk a few feet straight ahead and turn right onto the Yellow Trail and white-blazed side trail. Look up and take a short side trip to the 996-foot ridge top with magnificent views of the Ramapo Mountains, the distant Palisades, and Manhattan. This is another perfect spot to take a break and relax. Your hiking buddy will enjoy the breeze.

Take the orange- and yellow-blazed trails until they separate in about 100 feet, then follow the orange Schuber as it descends through a grove of mountain laurel. The trail here was designed to keep you and your pooch out of the swamp. It soon picks up an old woods road. At an intersection, the yellow-silver-blazed Yellow-Silver Trail begins and the orange blazes shoot off to the right. Go straight ahead onto the Yellow-Silver Trail for about 100 yards, then turn right onto the Yellow Trail that goes through woods that are cool and shady in summer and wind-protected in winter. Artifacts remain from the days of mining and later early camp days, such as a metal horse trough, kitchenware, and stone farmhouse ruins.

At the tree with yellow blazes and also the white blazes of the Millstone Trail loop, go right onto the Millstone with white blazes only for a downhill walk through the camp, past cabins and the Fox Brook, which tumbles out of Lake Vreeland. Walk across the lake's causeway back to the road and turn left onto the Schuber Trail back to the car. You and your dog will sleep well.

15. Hacklebarney Loop

Round-trip: 3 miles
Elevation range: 440–680 feet
Difficulty: Easy to moderate
Hiking time: 2 hours
Best canine hiking season: Year-round
Regulations: Dogs must be leashed
Maps: USGS Chester and Gladstone, NJ quadrangles; NJDEP Hacklebarney State Park
Information: Hacklebarney State Park, (908) 879-5677 in summer; c/o Voorhees State Park, (908) 638-6969 year-round; *www.njparksandforests.org*

Getting there: Take US Highway 206 to County Route 513 South/24 West (West Main Street) in Chester. At 1.3 miles, turn left onto State Park Road. At the Hacklebarney Cider Mill, make a right onto Hacklebarney Road. Drive for a winding 2.4 miles to this hidden jewel. The park entrance is on the left.

This hike is all your dog ever wanted encapsulated in one area. It has a little bit of everything for a dog—flat, rounded boulders left by the Wisconsin Glacier to hop from one to the next, two wild trout streams and an energetic river to quench even the slightest thirst, dramatic ravines for a change of pace, swaths of wildflowers to sniff, waterfalls, and wide trails and rocky paths to scramble. Your dog will also enjoy sunning after a dip, while you relax on perfectly placed benches on rock ledges over the Black River. This is a fun park—well designed by nature and humans in a small space.

Differently named short trails comprise this easy-to-follow loop. Take the white-blazed Main Trail to the right of the park office. Turn left onto the red-blazed Upper Trail that heads down the stone stairway and crosses

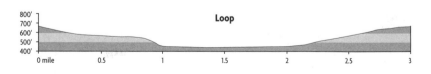

The Black River bisects a glacially carved hemlock ravine.

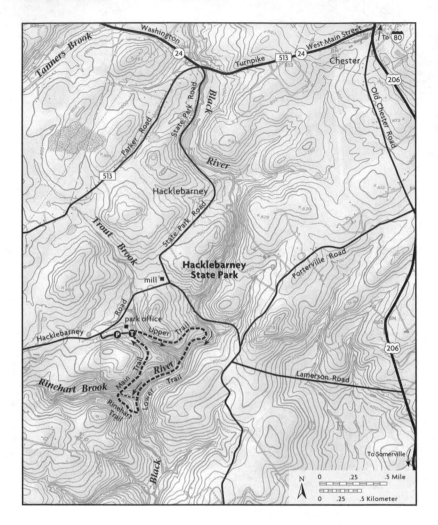

Trout Brook into deciduous forest on a macadam path. The brook's waterfalls and boulders beg for Bowser's exploration, easily accessed via a short path or stone steps.

The trail rises and falls with just enough climbing to give your dog some aerobic exercise. Strategically placed benches, right where you both want them, await on hilltops. An observant engineer hiked this path.

On the downhill into a ravine, you hear the Black River before you see it. This is a state-designated 465-acre Natural Area preserved for its special resources and habitats that support endangered and threatened species such as the wood turtle, barred owl, and Cooper's hawk. The trail, now the Lower Trail, bears right along the river over outcrops, ledges, and boulders under a cool hemlock canopy.

Stay next to the river and cross Trout Brook again and, about 1 mile later, Rinehart Brook on wooden bridges. The trail, now Rinehart Trail, heads uphill and joins the white-blazed Main Trail back to the parking lot.

This park has all the elements of a fun hike. Bring your fishing pole and license and have a lazy afternoon with your best pal. Pack a snack for you and your dog to enjoy while sitting on a flat boulder or at a picnic table.

16. Jockey Hollow: Primrose Brook Loop

Round-trip: 1.2 miles
Elevation range: 460–560 feet
Difficulty: Easy
Hiking time: 1 hour
Best canine hiking season: Year-round
Regulations: Dogs must be leashed; fee
Maps: USGS Mendham, NJ quadrangle; NY-NJTC North Kittatinny
   Trails Map 17, Morristown National Historical Park–Jockey Hol-
   low Unit and New Jersey Brigade
Information: Morristown National Historical Park, (973) 543-4030,
   www.nps.gov/morr

Getting there: From Interstate 287, take exit 30B in Harding Township. Turn west and then right at the first light onto US Highway 202. About 2 miles later, turn left onto Tempe Wick Road. Park at the Jockey Hollow Visitor Center. Pick up a map and pay a small entrance fee good for seven days. Drive through the park to the parking lot. Follow Cemetery Road and turn right onto Grand Parade Road and right again onto Jockey Hollow Road to the parking lot 0.3 mile on the right.

This is an easy walk for human and dog on a hillside along a moving stream. The trail crosses the stream in seven places, and there is always a great spot for Spot to get cool. This popular park is a joy in winter too, and your dog will enjoy a short walk in the snow.

Cross the road and scoot down onto the red-dot trail through the Primrose Brook floodplain. Boardwalks cover the wetter parts of the trail that traverses open, sunny woods to shady forest. The path rises and falls slightly, just enough to keep you and your dog in shape, following the side of Mount Kemble and moving away from the brook.

At a fork in the path, a sign offers long and short routes. Go right for the long loop of 1.2 miles. The path crosses the brook on large stepping-stones, and runs along Patriot's Path, Morris County's green corridor, for a short distance.

This is an ideal walk on a warm summer day. It is short, shady, and the brook is never too far to take your dog for a quick dip. Birdsong fills the open woods, and the trail twists and curves for a canine's hiking interest. This hike passes near George Washington's troop encampments during the Revolutionary War.

Farley chills in the Primrose Brook. It is a newly discovered favorite.

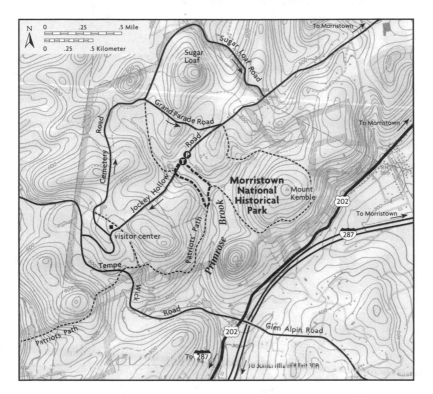

17. Merrill Creek Reservoir: Perimeter Trail

Round-trip: 5.5 miles
Elevation range: 900–1000 feet
Difficulty: Moderate
Hiking time: 4 hours
Best canine hiking season: Year-round
Regulations: Dogs must be leashed
Maps: USGS Bloomsbury, NJ quadrangle; Merrill Creek Reservoir
Information: Merrill Creek Reservoir, (908) 454-1213,
www.merrillcreek.com

Getting there: From County Route 519 in Union Town, turn right onto
Fox Farm Road for 5.5 miles. Turn right onto Richline Road for 0.6 mile,

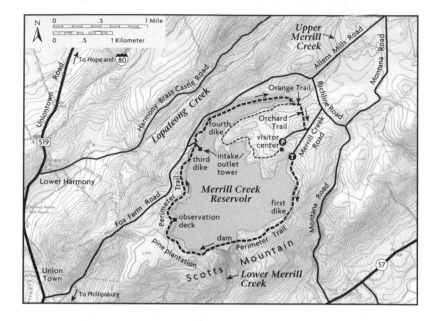

then go right again onto Merrill Creek Road for 0.3 mile to the parking lot and visitor center.

You and your dog will enjoy the very different terrain at Merrill Creek Reservoir on Scotts Mountain. The Perimeter Trail passes over dikes and dams with great views of the 650-acre reservoir, in and out of deciduous and evergreen woods, over a fresh, running creek, alongside meadows, and through an old orchard. Your dog will enjoy the sight and scent of a variety of wildlife on this 2000-acre property. Keep a close leash. This is an exciting hike for a dog.

If you want to see the taxidermy displays of local wildlife in the visitor center, hike during cool weather for dogs must remain in the car.

Take the black Perimeter Trail down through the woods to the boat ramp. Follow a wide gravel road through the closed gate, through deciduous woods, and over the first dike with a refreshing view of the water, then into the woods again.

The trail descends nicely onto the 0.5-mile-long main dam with Lower Merrill Creek, the reservoir's outlet, on the left. The tall, bare boles of a now-dead 1930s red pine plantation appear on the left. The trail turns right onto a footpath under the shady pines, a relief for your dog. Various trails appear, but always stay close to the lake.

At the top of a rise, you can rest on a bench where, in winter, you can see through the trees to the lake. Turn right into the woods and take a detour downhill to the observation deck. Look to the left to spot a pair of bald eagles that nest here year-round. Back on the trail, a 2.5-mile marker signals one of many stone walls, from long-ago farms, that ramble around the property.

The trail crosses the third dike, heads to the left of a parking lot, and then goes through a gate onto a gravel road through a meadow of flying grasshoppers that will enchant your dog as much as you.

Soon cross a fourth dike. At 4 miles, the path becomes dark and cool under a dense hemlock canopy with a north woods feel. Cross Upper Merrill Creek on a footbridge, then turn left onto the Orange Trail for 250 feet. Turn right onto the green-blazed Orchard Trail. Go through a gate and cross the road, hiking through woods and between fields and hedgerows where deer lurk, feasting on Eve's fruit. You and Fido will see the animals if you are quiet. The path takes you back to the visitor center.

Merrill Creek Reservoir is private property, open to the public seven days a week. The grounds are closed during an orange national security alert or higher. Check the website or call the office to check.

Great blue heron

Eagles nest year-round at Merrill Creek Reservoir.

18. Pyramid Mountain Loop

Round-trip: 4 miles
Elevation range: 640–860 feet
Difficulty: Moderate to difficult
Hiking time: 2.5 hours
Best canine hiking season: Spring, summer, fall
Regulations: Dogs must be leashed
Maps: USGS Boonton, NJ quadrangle; Morris County Park Commission Pyramid Mountain Natural Historic Area
Information: Pyramid Mountain Natural Historic Area, (973) 334-3130; *www.morrisparks.net*

Getting there: From State Route 23, turn onto Boonton Avenue (County Route 511) in Butler and drive 4.4 miles to the parking lot on the right.

This hike takes Fido on rocky uphills, downhill rock scrambles, stream crossings, and some of the most impressive glacial boulders in the state. Make sure your dog has tough pads to handle the steep rock scrambles and is in shape to handle the uphills. Humans should wear boots with good ankle support. Bring plenty of water.

The Blue Trail leads out from the parking lot in two places. Take either path and cross Stony Brook, a rushing stream in spring and a trickle in summer. Turn right onto the Yellow Trail at its start and head steadily uphill. The path is rocky all the way and can be a heart-pumper even for an in-shape canine. After a climb to the ridge top, the Blue Trail comes in from the left and joins the Yellow for a short distance until you take it to the right, leaving the Yellow Trail on the left.

At about 0.2 mile, the Blue Trail goes off to the left, but you take the White Trail straight ahead to the altarlike mountaintop where Tripod Rock (also known as Three Pillar Rock) rests at 806 feet.

Geologists and land surveyors debate the origin of this rock arrangement. Geologists say glacial action left this boulder balancing on three smaller ones. Land surveyors say it is an ancient travel marker along a "ley line," a straight line of many such tripod rocks that once marked

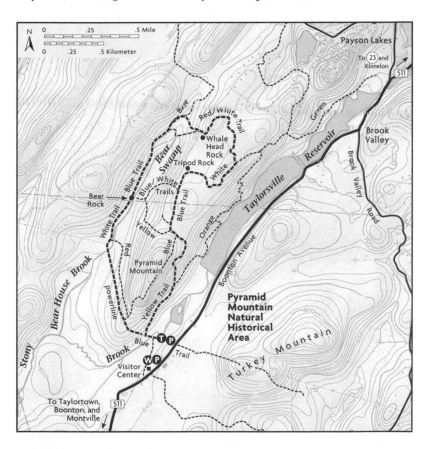

travel routes through the forests for traders and others. They occur all over the eastern seaboard. On the western side of the ridge, two stones are an ancient calendar marking the summer solstice as the sun sets between them in late June.

Continue on the White Trail for about 0.4 mile, then turn left onto the Red/White Trail downhill toward Whale Head Rock. The trail is rocky with ups and downs through woods and eventually comes out into a sunny area, where red/white blazes indicate that the trail turns left. Turn left onto a wide, obvious trail over rock set into roots and moss like a mosaic. It soon becomes a downhill rock scramble. At the bottom, bear right and cross the stream over rocks. Your dog will enjoy the new sensation and challenge.

The Yellow Trail is a fun climb over rock slabs and roots.

Turn left onto the Blue Trail alongside Bear Swamp. Your dog will love its primal feel and scent, and a step into swamp soil will cool his feet on hot days. Hike on to Bear Rock, one of the largest glacial erratics in the state. Bear right onto the White Trail along Bear House Brook and out into a sunny powerline right-of-way. At another junction of the Blue Trail, head to the right. Continue on the Blue, past the Yellow, and back to Stony Brook.

19. Terrace Pond

Round-trip: 4.5 miles
Elevation range: 1140–1440 feet
Difficulty: Difficult
Hiking time: 4 hours
Best canine hiking season: Year-round
Regulations: Dogs must be leashed; carry out dog waste
Maps: USGS Wawayanda, NJ quadrangle; NY-NJTC North Jersey
    Trails Map 116; NJDEP Wawayanda State Park
Information: Wawayanda State Park, (973) 853-4462,
    www.njparksandforests.org

Getting there: From State Route 23 in West Milford, take Clinton Road for 7.5 miles. The parking lot is on the left, directly across the road from the Yellow and Blue trailheads. If you drive past it and go to the second parking lot across from the pipeline right-of-way, you have gone too far.

This rugged trail offers a variety of dramatic terrain, passing through mountain laurel and towering hemlock and hardwoods, over rock scrambles, and across stream and wetland crossings on planks and rock to a glistening glacial pond at the top. It is a fun agility course for the experienced canine hiker. Bring plenty of water.

Cross the road and take the Blue Trail to the left on a rock, moss, and roots footpath under open forest, scented and softened with evergreen needles. Trail maintenance crews built a large stepping-stone path over a wet area of fern, laurel, and sweet pepperbush that perfumes the August air. The beauty of this trail resembles a garden.

At 0.5 mile, the path turns right onto a steep, sunny pipeline, becoming slatey rock. Stay to the right to see blue blazes painted on rock on the

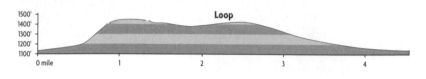

ground at 0.5 mile that indicate the correct path into the woods.

The trail steadily climbs, winding around and over lichen-covered boulders, some requiring shimmying and sliding. A short-legged Fido may need a hand up. A rounded cliff of purple puddingstone, a quartz-speckled sandstone, offers a fun climb and breeze for all with a northern view of the Kittatinny Ridge and New York mountains.

The Blue Trail intersects the White Trail that circles Terrace Pond on top of Bearfort Mountain, a state-designated Natural Area. Head to the right and take a break on the slanted rock cliffs that enclose the 2.5-acre

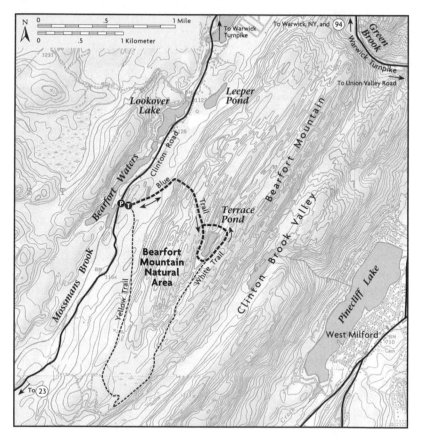

Slabs of puddingstone and sweet pepperbush dip down to crystalline Terrace Pond, a mountaintop gem.

pond. Enjoy the sweet air and cooling breeze, but keep your dog out of this sparkling water where no swimming is allowed.

Back on the trail, watch for the white blazes that lead slightly away from the pond. The trail leads through massive rhododendron and dense shrubbery and over outcrops. At the far end of the pond, your canine pal may need help scaling down a rock chute. Cross a wetland on planks where tiny pipewort blooms among tall ferns.

The White path meets the Blue. Turn right onto it and head back the way you came.

20. Schooley's Mountain: Boulder Gorge Loop

Round-trip: 3.3 miles

Elevation range: 580–1000 feet

Difficulty: Moderate with a difficult climb

Hiking time: 2.5 hours

Best canine hiking season: Spring, summer, fall

Regulations: Dogs must be leashed

Maps: USGS Hackettstown, NJ quadrangle; Morris County Park
Commission, Schooley's Mountain County Park

Information: Morris County Park Commission, (973) 326-7600,
www.morrisparks.net

Getting there: From US Highway 206 in Chester, take State Route 24 West
(County Route 513 South). At 4.5 miles, in the little town of Long Valley,
turn right with Route 24 (County Route 517 and Schooley's Mountain
Road). Make an immediate right turn onto Fairview Avenue and drive
for 1.8 miles to the parking lot on the right.

This is an exciting hike along a dramatic glacial stream gorge with tons
of boulders that have tumbled down the mountain. Your dog will enjoy
the wet scents and sensations of the Electric Brook where, even in summer, there is water. A lot of little waterfalls and quiet pools will keep Fido
busy, and the hike down the mountain is easy on the Patriots' Path.

Cross the street and enter the woods at the wooden signpost for Patriots' Path, a white-blazed trail that traverses much of Morris County,
connecting many federal, state, county, and municipal green spaces.

Patriots' Path immediately bears left, heading slowly up Schooley's
Mountain. At 0.5 mile, go left onto the unblazed Boulder Gorge Trail on
a steep downhill.

In a few hundred feet, the trail turns to the right on a flat, wide, mossy
path that leads to an interesting rock cliff—perhaps an old quarry. After
a heavy spring rain, it must be quite dramatic.

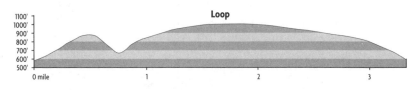

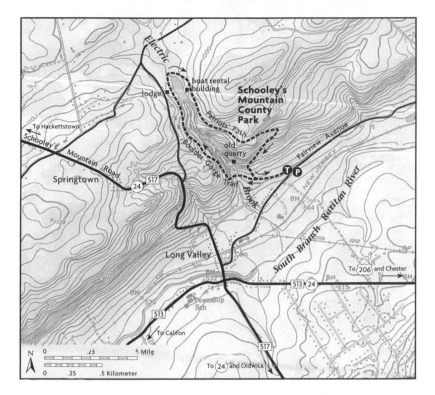

Back on the trail, a cairn indicates that the trail turns left, heading downhill over rock steps. Cross a dirt road and Electric Brook. Turn right for a scenic, steep climb beside an impressive stream. At the top of the hill, you and your canine pal can take a side trail down to the falls and quiet pool. You can also take a break on a great rock that overhangs the falls and watch the stream tumbling over smaller falls upstream. There are plenty of play spots for Fido and you along this watery wonder.

Uphill, a side trail shoots to the left, but you go straight along the stream over a flat rock scramble—a different terrain for a dog. The trail bears slightly left here, but follow the water and take a quick excursion out on the wooden bridge over the dam for your dog's sensory pleasure.

Back on the trail, see the lodge to the left. Hike alongside the pond and cross it on the next walkway. Go past the boat rental building, up the manicured lawn, past the buildings on the right to take the white-blazed Patriots' Path back down the mountain. The path starts out paved, becoming gravel and then a dirt footpath as it turns right into the woods.

Follow the white blazes 0.5 mile down to a view of Long Valley's

A fascinating moment watching the Electric Brook falls on the Boulder Gorge Trail

farms and 0.6 mile more to the parking lot on Fairview Avenue. This is a great hike.

21. Bearfort Ridge: Surprise Lake Loop

Round-trip: 5 miles
Elevation range: 820–1300 feet
Difficulty: Moderate with a strenuous climb
Hiking time: 3.5 hours
Best canine hiking season: Year-round
Regulations: Dogs must be on a 6-foot leash; carry out trash
Maps: USGS Greenwood Lake, NY quadrangle; NY-NJTC North Jersey Trails Map 116; NJDEP Abram S. Hewitt State Forest
Information: Wawayanda State Park, (973) 853-4462, *www.njparksandforests.org*

Getting there: From State Route 23 in Hamburg, turn onto State Route 94 North, drive 12.3 miles and turn right onto Warwick Turnpike (County Route 21) in Warwick, New York. Drive 7.3 miles to a small parking lot immediately beyond a bridge on the north side of the road.

This fresh, verdant trail in fall and winter brings you and your canine pal the gift of woodland detail and sights to see without the distraction of leaves. Bold rocks, streams, and shallow soil become the substrate for lush growth of bright green moss, lichen, fern, rhododendron, mountain laurel, hemlock, and pine. It's a green hike with great views, adventure in unusual habitats, waterfalls, lunch on a sunny ridge top, speckled rock, and trees growing out of boulders. The Bearfort Ridge Natural Area is home to the endangered red-shouldered hawk and the timid Eastern timber rattler. Your experienced dog will love the streams, varied habitats with distinctive aromas, and path like an agility course. This hike is among the cream!

Walk east about 50 feet, cross a creek, and turn left into the woods at a sign for the Jeremy Glick Trail, heading up through rhododendron. Soon see the white-blazed Bearfort Ridge Trail that starts with a steep climb. Turn left, hiking briefly through hemlock on an undulating trail, crossing several streams and climbing boulders. When you almost reach the top, turn around for a view to the southwest.

Climb steeply to a relatively flat hemlock grove with a huge mound of puddingstone on the left. You will be rewarded with views of Manhattan, Bearfort Ridge, and a bit of Upper Greenwood Lake. Then, a steep rock scramble—Fido may need a leg up—and a ridge of upturned rock with pitch pine and scrub oak will test your and your dog's leg muscles.

At the top, pitch pine and young hemlock flank the path like a wild garden. Fungi adorn boulders; ferns decorate rocks and logs. Bare trees bring the smallest forest goodies into focus. Scents for Fido abound, and a good nose can lead the way.

The ridge undulates through swamps with blueberry, over streams, then up rock scrambles to views of Upper Greenwood Lake. To the left, an Atlantic white cedar swamp at about 1300 feet appears below you. On the edge of the trail, notice the split rock wall that has eroded and stands apart from the mountain.

At the top of a knoll, the Bearfort Ridge Trail ends and meets the yellow-blazed Ernest Walter Trail. Surprise Lake is ahead of you. Go right onto the Ernest Walter Trail and head downhill to a swamp and stream

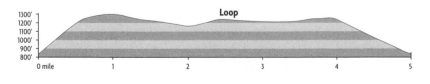

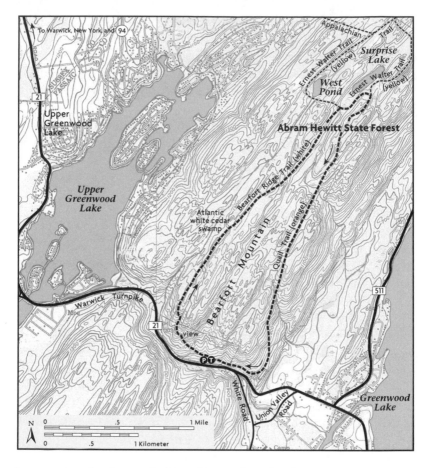

in protective bruin-type habitat. Enjoy a bit of rock, root, and hummock hopping across the stream, a ramble through a rhododendron thicket, then a short tromp to Surprise Lake.

Head back on the Ernest Walter Trail, then turn left onto the orange-blazed Quail Trail, an old woods road that slides gradually down the mountain through rocky streambeds, swamps, and stream crossings that make this hike an adventure. Prepare to wade across if necessary. Always watch for the infrequent blazes. This trail rambles below the ridge, giving the hiker and dog some extra treats—sparkling little waterfalls that cascade from ridge-top boulders.

Enjoy these rich evergreen woods. Wear waterproof boots and carry a hiking stick. Your dog will have a great time.

22. Columbia Trail: High Bridge to Ken Lockwood Gorge

Round-trip: 7 miles
Elevation range: Flat
Difficulty: Moderate
Hiking time: 3.5 hours
Best canine hiking season: Year-round
Regulations: Dogs must be leashed
Maps: USGS High Bridge, NJ quadrangle; Hunterdon County Department of Parks and Recreation Columbia Trail
Information: County of Hunterdon, Department of Parks and Recreation, (908) 782-1158, *www.co.hunterdon.nj.us*

Getting there: From State Route 31 North at High Bridge, turn right onto County Route 513 North into town. At 1 mile, turn left into "The Commons" municipal parking lot on Main Street (County Route 513).

This hike traverses a defunct railbed through the town of High Bridge to Ken Lockwood Gorge and the South Branch of the Raritan River. It offers you and your dog either a relaxed or an energetic hike above dramatic terrain.

Walk across Main Street to the trailhead. The paved trail crosses several streets, then turns to gravel as it runs past Lake Solitude and above country for a bird's-eye view of houses in the woods. Soon you and your dog will leave the town behind and hear only the river and birds. The river weaves near, then out of view, but remains identifiable by the faint swath of white-barked American sycamore that lines its banks. Cross a bridge over Cokesbury Road at 1.2 miles as you and Fido chug your way to the gorge.

As you hike through a rock cut with a hillside of ferns and the river on the other side, it is easy to imagine the defunct Central Railroad of New Jersey hauling iron ore and passengers to their destination in Morris County. At 2.5 miles, cross the bridge over the river and the gorge. Side trails take you down to the river, if you can find them.

Soon, the teal-diamond-blazed Highlands Trail joins the Columbia from the woods on the left and stays with you. On a rock wall to the right, a great natural rock garden exists with ferns, mosses, and tiny trailing plants growing from crevices, even in winter. There is a serenity in the woods when the trees have tossed their leaves off and present to the hiker a gift of long views over valley and river, notches and hillside—close-up treasures unencumbered by green frills.

Turn around at the 3.5-mile mark and go back the way you came.

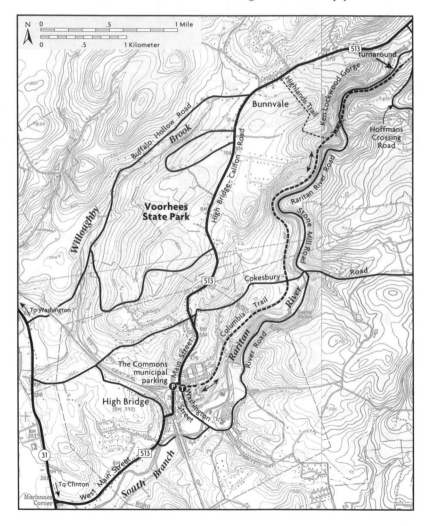

The Columbia Trail twists above dramatic Ken Lockwood Gorge and the South Branch of the Raritan River.

23. Lake Marguerite–Griffith Woods Loop

Round-trip: 2.5 miles
Elevation range: 640–720 feet
Difficulty: Easy
Hiking time: 1.5 hours
Best canine hiking season: Year-round
Regulations: Dogs must be leashed; carry out trash
Maps: USGS Belvidere, NJ quadrangle; Washington Township Recreation Commission, Lake Marguerite Wildlife Refuge and Griffith Woods Natural Area
Information: Washington Township, Warren County, (908) 689-7200, *www.washington-twp-warren.org*

Getting there: From the intersection of State Routes 57 and 31 in Washington, drive 1.2 miles west on Route 57 and turn right at the light onto

Lorraine and Shadoe out for their usual fun in Griffith Woods.

Brass Castle Road (County Route 623). Drive 1.8 miles and turn right onto Jonestown Road. The parking lot is on the left.

The 22-acre Lake Marguerite Wildlife Refuge and 44-acre Griffith Woods Natural Area, both once private estates, are true gifts to human and canine hikers to be kept in their natural states in perpetuity. You and your dog will enjoy a short trip around a lake and a hike through almost-pristine woods. A number of streams crisscross the woods with wooden bridges—some on trails and some as side excursions just for fun. Your dog can keep his feet moist and stay cool here during our hot summers. Also superb when the ground is covered in snow, this hike is far from the crowds for a venture in quiet nature. These are very sweet woods.

Walk through the gate on an old farm road along a meadow and woods. Lake Marguerite is before you. Bear left and follow the path three-quarters of the way around the lake on a raised levee over feeder streams and continue to bear left into the woods. A sign directs you to the Red Trail.

Turn left onto the path and cross over a stream on a wooden bridge, still on Lake Marguerite land. Follow the footpath to the left of the stream and head toward the red blaze. You are now in Griffith Woods. Turn left and follow the Red Trail through deciduous woods with a full understory of musclewood and spicebush, fragrant in spring.

Watch the blazes here when snow or leaves cover the path. Follow the Red Trail around the perimeter of the woods, hugging low stone walls with farm fields on the other side of a hedgerow. After a bridge crossing, the White Trail cuts across the woods along a stream, connecting the north and south sides of the Red Trail. Hike the White for a while for an

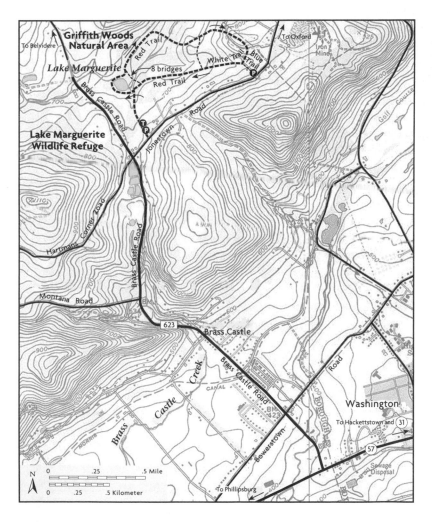

extra bit of fun, but come back to the Red again. Many old trees live here among the regenerating American beech saplings. The path rises through a red cedar stand, then ambles along a switchback for a slight climb.

Turn right at the 1-mile marker on a tulip poplar. The Blue Trail turns left heading to the road, but ignore it and continue straight. The raised path traverses wetland and bridges, but you may need to hop some rocks over narrow rivulets.

Follow the path back to Lake Marguerite and back to your car. The township is looking for volunteers to help maintain these trails.

24. Mahlon Dickerson Reservation: Pine Swamp Loop

Round-trip: 5 miles, including overlook
Elevation range: 1200–1388 feet
Difficulty: Moderate
Hiking time: 2.5 hours
Best canine hiking season: Year-round
Regulations: Dogs must be leashed
Maps: USGS Franklin, NJ quadrangle; Morris County Park Commission, Mahlon Dickerson Reservation
Information: Morris County Park Commission, (973) 326-7600, *www.morrisparks.net*

Getting there: From State Route 15 in Jefferson, take Weldon Road for 3.9 miles to the parking lot/picnic area on the left.

This hike through swamp and upland crosses streams and seeps, and passes through tunnels of mountain laurel, encountering a lot of critter tracks in winter and plenty of variety to keep Fido interested and cool.

Go straight across the parking lot onto the teal-diamond-blazed Highlands Trail. The paved path soon becomes dirt. At the T, turn right with

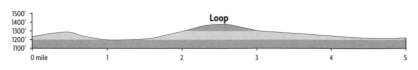

Streams, like this tributary of the Rockaway River on the Pine Swamp Trail, sparkle up the winter landscape for a great hike.

the Highlands onto the Pine Swamp Trail, blazed white. Hike downhill through deciduous woods and cross a creek, part of the Rockaway River drainage. Tributaries of three watersheds originate from this 3300-acre reservation: the Musconetcong, which flows west to the Delaware River; the Wallkill, which runs north to the Hudson; and the Rockaway, which flows southeast to Newark Bay. There's plenty of water to keep your dog cool.

American basswood grows in the upland part of the trail. In spring, its blossoms perfume the woods.

As the trail nears a road, it splits. Stay left. At a trail junction where a green trail begins to the left, continue right onto the white and teal trail. As you head down the north slope, more evergreens appear. Cross another tributary and pass through a mountain laurel grove that blooms in late May to early June. At a Y intersection, go left and watch for blazes.

Blue jays, the eyes of the forest, flit through the trees. The path crosses the swamp and a spring-fed run where human and canine can enjoy a little boulder hopping, especially great for your dog in summer. Cross streams and seeps; duck under tunnels of pink laurel.

At a junction, the teal Highlands Trail goes right and you go left on white. An overlook of a small section of Pine Swamp appears on the left. White pine was once the dominant tree here, but after being heavily logged it didn't regenerate. Now hardwoods, hemlock, and rhododendron mimic a northern forest. This swamp is a component of the core preservation area of the Highlands. Five minutes later, the trail cuts through the edge of the main swamp on your right.

The woods are full of animal tracks in the snow—bear, mouse, squirrel, mole, and possibly coyote. A bridle trail leads off to the right, but you go left unless you'd like to make a longer loop with several possibilities.

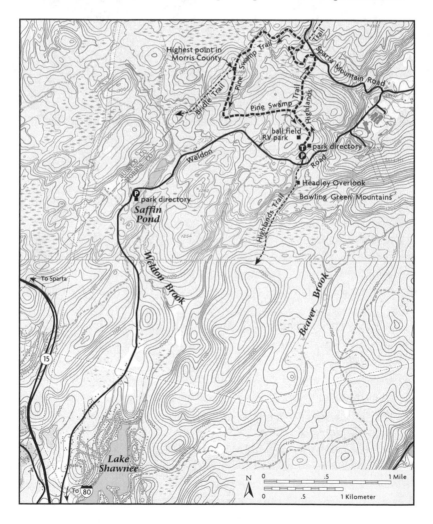

Staying on the white Pine Swamp Trail, reach the highest point in Morris County at 1395 feet and see Bowling Green Mountain through the trees. Turn left at the T intersection. At a junction of the green- and white-blazed trails, turn right on white and head back to the parking lot.

Tired after the hike? Have a snack on a comfortable outcrop, just ten minutes across the street with a nice view to Lake Hopatcong. The trail picks up at the directory. Cross the road and head into the woods on the teal Highlands Trail. Turn left to Headley Overlook at the sign for "OVERLOOK."

This parking lot has a kiosk with trail maps and a doggy water fountain from mid-April to October.

25. Norvin Green Vista Circuit

Round-trip: 5 miles
Elevation range: 580–1040 feet
Difficulty: Difficult
Hiking time: 4 hours
Best canine hiking season: Year-round
Regulations: Dogs must be on a 6-foot leash and under the immediate control of the owner at all times
Maps: USGS Wanaque, NJ Quadrangle; NY-NJTC, North Jersey Trails 115
Information: Norvin Green State Forest, managed by Ringwood State Park, (973) 962-7031, *www.njparksandforests.org*

Getting there: From State Route 23 North in West Milford, turn right onto Germantown Road. At a T intersection, turn right onto Macopin Road. In 0.2 mile, turn left onto Weaver Road. Drive 0.8 mile and turn right onto Otter Hole Road. The second small parking lot with a sign for Bloomingdale is 0.5 mile on the left. From Route 23 South, take the jughandle onto Echo Lake Road and turn right onto Macopin Road. Follow same directions.

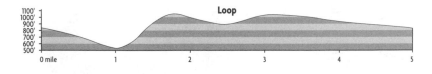

This hike is one of the best. The trail traverses two vistas with great views, boulders and rock slabs to climb, ridges, streams and falls, and plant tunnels, making this an exciting and adventuresome hike for experienced canines only.

Take the blue-blazed Hewitt-Butler Trail. Cross a moving stream through a mixed oak forest. At a junction where the green Otter Hole Trail comes in from the left and the teal-diamond-blazed Highlands Trail joins the blue, turn right onto blue and teal. Boulder hop across a wide stream with waterfalls, climb a short hill, scoot along a ridge, then descend, meeting the yellow-blazed Wyanokie Crest Trail briefly, to reach a confluence of streams.

After crossing a stream, the trail bends left, but go straight a short while to see Chikahoki Falls, which looks like a rapid in the Colorado. Retrace your steps to the trail. Now at 600 feet, the trail climbs to Carris Hill at 1040 feet. Watch for blazes as the trail zigzags up through saplings scattered among dead trees on a false summit, then rises strenuously through mountain laurel and over slabs of smooth rock.

You'll know Carris Hill by the panoramic view of mountains, the three yellow blazes, and its name painted on rock.

Taking a break on Carris Hill. Winter hiking can really warm you up.

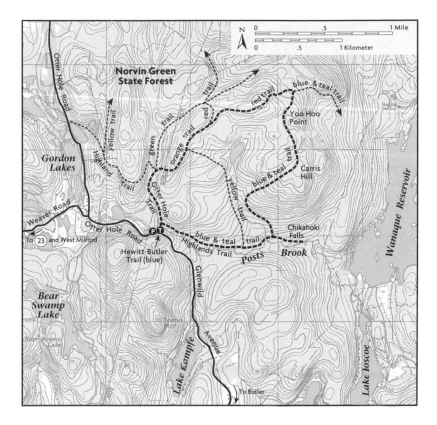

Slide down a rock slab to the trail and continue on to Yoo Hoo Point at 1000 feet. See the bald pate of High Point across a short distance. Turn left onto the red-blazed Wyanokie Circular Trail, leaving the Highlands and blue, scooting down through mountain laurel tunnels.

See a tripod rock on the left just before turning left onto the orange trail, which is more gold in color. Cross a rock slab to a T intersection where three orange blazes appear on rock, signaling the end of the orange trail. The yellow trail crosses in front of you. Turn right onto yellow. Don't get confused with yellow and orange.

Come to the edge of the woods on a cliff overlooking a ravine. Head down into the ravine and cross the stream. At a sign to the Otter Hole parking lot, the yellow trail continues straight, but turn left onto the green Otter Hole Trail. At the end of the green trail, the Highlands Trail goes left, but turn right and cross the creek with waterfalls, soon reaching the parking lot.

26. Point Mountain Riverwalk Loop

Round-trip: 3.2–3.7 miles
Elevation range: 420–560 feet; 935 feet for extended hike
Difficulty: Easy to moderate
Hiking time: 1.5–2.5 hours
Best canine hiking season: Year-round
Regulations: Dogs must be leashed
Maps: USGS Washington, NJ quadrangle; Hunterdon County Dept. of Parks and Recreation, Point Mountain Reservation
Information: County of Hunterdon Department of Parks and Recreation, (908) 782-1158, *www.co.hunterdon.nj.us*

Getting there: From State Route 57 south of Hackettstown, take a left onto Penwell Road and go across the Musconetcong River and 0.5 mile to the parking lot on the right.

This hike offers you and your dog a fast, easy hike in the woods along a small, boulder-dotted river. Mountain streams, wineberry in summer, gentle terrain, and the river make this hike in the Musconetcong Mountain Range soul-filling. Your dog will enjoy the wild feel.

Take the orange Ridge Trail, a dirt road around the edges of farm fields toward Point Mountain. Turn right along the bottom of the fields. Enter the woods at the corner of the field and take the blue Riverwalk Trail that traverses a New Jersey Fish and Wildlife Trout Conservation Area for a short distance. The path crosses an intermittent stream and then sidles along the banks of the Musconetcong.

Just out of state land, the Riverwalk Trail splits. Turn right and stay close to the river filled with tumbled boulders and rocks.

The trail crosses Point Mountain Road. Ignore the orange blazes and stay with blue beside the river. The path begins to move away from the river, narrowing to begin its loop back. Watch for blazes—there are no doubles here to indicate a turn. Roses and wineberry get thick near the

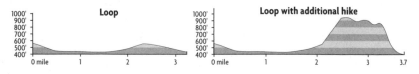

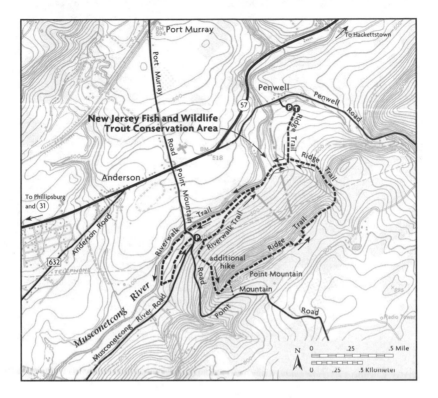

trail here, where it is less maintained with a wilder feel although it travels between the river and Musconetcong River Road.

A plight shared by most central and southern New Jersey parks is the lack of personnel to maintain trails. Park naturalists do announce special days to come to the woods for a bit of housekeeping on weekends, and they hope for volunteers.

Now on the back side of the loop, the forest is early successional with black cherry, sassafras, American sycamore, and a full understory of dogwood, witch hazel, viburnum, and musclewood. Along the path are two large holes in the ground that may have been iron pits.

Cross the road; turn right onto the blue Riverwalk Trail and head uphill. The blue turns left onto an old logging road. You always know where the river is by the tall, well-branched white American sycamores that grow from its banks. The path angles back to the river and the beginning of the loop. At an orange blaze on a cut log, blue goes left but you go straight uphill, across the creek, and out onto the farm field to the Riverwalk Trail again. Turn left uphill to your car.

You can hike another half-mile to a viewpoint on Point Moun and create a larger loop. After crossing Point Mountain Road on the way back, keep right on the orange Ridge Trail instead of the blue, and hike steeply up to the overlook. From here you can see to the Delaware Water Gap on a clear day. Continue on the orange trail across the hillside back to your car.

27. Tourne Park

Round-trip: 1.5 mile
Elevation range: 600–897 feet
Difficulty: Easy
Hiking time: 1 hour
Best canine hiking season: Year-round
Regulations: Dogs must be leashed
Maps: USGS Boonton, NJ quadrangle; Morris County Park Commission, Tourne County Park
Information: Morris County Park Commission, (973) 326-7600, *www.morrisparks.net*

Getting there: From Interstate 80 East take exit 38 (Denville), or exit 39 from Interstate 80 West, onto US Highway 46 East. At 1.7 miles, turn left onto Boulevard. Drive 3.2 miles and bear left at the fork onto Powerline Road. At 0.8 mile, turn left onto McCaffrey Lane. The parking lot next to ball fields is 0.6 mile on the left.

Quick, easy to get to, and slightly cardio, this civilized hike is popular year-round among canines and humans. Great boulders adorn this almost-city park where wildlife such as the pileated woodpecker can

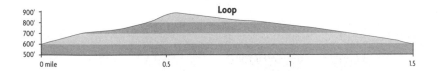

Opposite: The Musconetcong River flows 42 miles to the Delaware River. Many of its tributaries are trout production streams. It is destined to be designated the 169th National Wild and Scenic River.

be seen. Even in winter, families and a lot of dogs take this short but mighty hike to an accessible summit. A perfect after-work exercise, this is a "no-excuses" hike.

Cross the street to the wide gravel Decamp Trail, which circles steadily uphill to the "tourne," or summit, at 897 feet. Make a right at the fork. On the way up, views over the Rockaway Valley extend to the Rockaway River and Wildcat Ridge. There used to be views from the tourne itself, but now there are few.

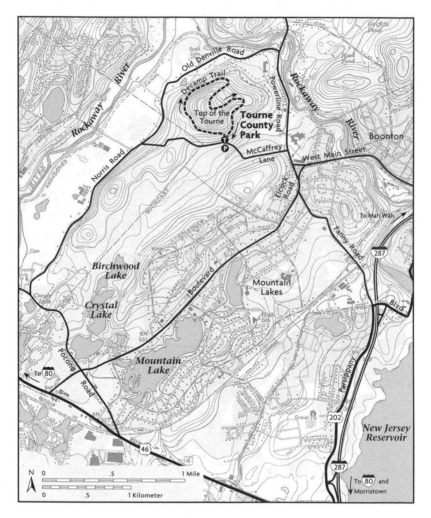

Visitors hike the "no excuses" Decamp Trail to the top of the tourne.

On the downhill, the gravel path through juniper and hardwoods takes you and your dog gently back to your car. You'll be glad you came.

THE CENTRAL PIEDMONT

Shale and sandstone lowlands, rolling terrain, and volcanic mountains characterize the Piedmont. Many people recognize the red dirt that streaks through New Brunswick. Called Brunswick shale and accounting for the preponderance of brick houses, it was deposited across the central part of the state about 225 million years ago by the ocean that covered the land. (New Jersey was inundated again and again over hundreds of millions of years before it became New Jersey.)

When North America drifted westward, central New Jersey was wet and murky with mudflats and swamps. Then, about 125 million years ago, lava flows created the three Watchung Mountains, while magma intrusions—underground lava that never broke through the earth's surface—formed the Palisades, Sourland Mountains, and Cushetunk Mountain, as well as some small hills scattered across the plains. The softer shale and sandstones weathered and eroded, causing the volcanic mountains to stand above the lowlands.

These varying mountains and plains with numerous rivers, streams, and lakes make the Piedmont a fun place for you and your dog to hike. Everything you might want in a hike—mountains, gentle hills, streams, or on the flat—is within reach. The Piedmont is a great place for novice hikers to get in shape. The trails are sociable and civilized. No excuses!

The Piedmont lowlands stretch 1000 miles from the Hudson River to Virginia with a few disconnected spots in Connecticut and Massachusetts.

28. Lord Stirling Stable Dog Walk

Round-trip: 2–3.2 miles
Elevation range: 220–260 feet
Difficulty: Moderate
Hiking time: 1 hour
Best canine hiking season: Year-round
Regulations: Dog fee; dogs must be leashed
Map: USGS Bernardsville, NJ quadrangle; Somerset County Park
    Commission Trail Map
Information: Lord Stirling Stable, (908) 766-5955,
    www.somersetcountyparks.org

Getting there: Take Interstate 287 to exit 30A (North Maple Avenue) into the town of Basking Ridge. At the first fork in the road, bear left onto South Maple Avenue for 0.75 mile to the stable on the left.

The Friends of Lord Stirling Stable dog walk happens every Saturday, rain, snow, or shine. Established in 1998, it has been canceled only once

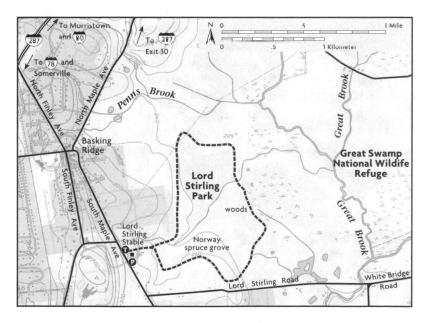

Every Saturday, canines and families hike the bridle trails at the Lord Stirling dog walk.

during a blizzard. When it snows, the maintenance crew plows a path to make the walk easier for all.

Dog walks are scheduled for either Saturday morning or evening, depending on the season. Their length depends on the day's leader and which group you fall into. Walkers find their own pace and spread into subgroups, always under the watch of trail-knowledgeable people.

From out of the gate, almost a hundred canines and humans take off up the bridle path at Lord Stirling Stable for an hour of exhilarating fun. This fast-paced sociable hike provides exercise and laughs for all, including families with children, even grandparents, on wide carriage roads and footpaths through a mix of habitat and terrain.

Don't miss out on any of the fun. Arrive a good half-hour beforehand to sign in, pay a nominal donation per dog (humans are free), and enjoy the interactions in the parking lot as dogs meet and greet, noses to tails. The staff reports no canine personality problems, perhaps because the stable grounds are no single dog's turf.

Once on the move, dogs get down to the business of the trail, first via a wide dirt road alongside horse pastures, then up a gradual incline to a hilltop grove of Norway spruce. The route becomes narrow, leading into mixed oak–hickory woods with American beech, follows cindered roads past meadows, emerges onto grassy paths beside wetlands, and crosses over streams.

The group eventually splits into two—those who zip and those who lag, be they dogs with short legs or slower people. Leisurely hikers can take one of many shortcuts back to the stable with the "sweep" who picks up the rear.

With 12 miles of equestrian trails on this 450-acre tract managed by the Somerset County Park Commission, the route changes every week depending on the leader's preferences, weather, and ground conditions. Numbered mounting blocks and named trails coordinate with a trail map obtained at the office. People who do the dog walk come from near and far to get away from the usual crowds, malls, and pavement and to socialize with other dog owners.

29. D&R Canal Towpath: Prallsville Mill and Lock to Lambertville

One-way: 4.2 miles
Elevation range: 100 feet flat and steady
Difficulty: Easy
Hiking time: 2 hours
Best canine hiking season: Year-round
Regulations: Dogs must be leashed; doggy bags provided
Maps: USGS Stockton, NJ quadrangle; NJDEP Delaware & Raritan Canal State Park
Information: Delaware & Raritan Canal State Park, (732) 873-3050, *www.dandrcanal.com; www.njparksandforests.org*

Getting there: Take County Route 29 to Lambertville. There are two parking lots. To reach the park's official parking lot, turn onto Bridge Street, then left into the Lambertville Station parking lot, just before the bridge, and drive down to the boat launch area. To avoid a weekend public parking fee, tell the attendant you are going to the state park. The other parking lot is next to Cavella Park on Mount Hope Street.

For two cars, drive farther north on County Route 29 to just above Stockton. Turn left into the almost-hidden parking lot just before the historic stone and wood buildings of the Prallsville Mill.

Take your dog for an easy, interesting hike along this abandoned railroad bed of the Belvidere-Delaware Railway Line. He will enjoy its diverse situations, such as standing on an aqueduct above a fun falls, swimming in the placid canal, and scouting the sights, sounds, and scents of this busy, mostly sunny, path that runs through two historic towns between the D&R Canal and the Delaware River. With just one car, hike a moderate out-and-back hike of 8.4 miles in 5 hours.

Once plied by mules and later by railroads, this 22-mile feeder canal flows south to the 44-mile main canal in Trenton. Memorabilia abounds, but your dog may be only interested in sniffing the old telegraph poles and tracks that form wildflower garden borders.

On the path starting at the Prallsville Mill turn left to head south on crushed stone with houses on the left and fields on the right. In 0.3 mile, cross the small streets of historic Stockton. Soon the path becomes a levee between the canal and the river.

At 2.7 miles, pass under US Highway 202 and turn left onto the gravel road to cross the canal, then right onto the sandy trail. Give your dog a break while you enjoy the scenery from a bench under a maple tree.

Kerri and Buster admire the D&R Canal from a defunct railbed on the trail.

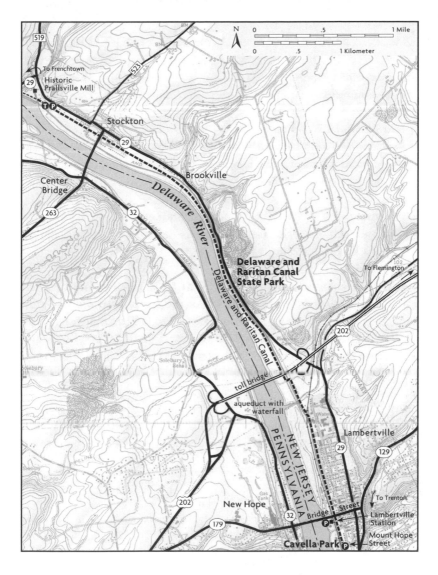

Fido's senses will all engage while crossing the canal again on a narrow footbridge over an aqueduct with a waterfall. Soon, at 4 miles, a massive American sycamore tree signals the city limits of Lambertville. As you pass backyards and gardens, follow a boardwalk under a railroad bridge remnant, and cross Bridge Street toward the Lambertville Lock. Your pal can get cool in the canal almost anywhere.

Retrace your route unless you have left a car.

30. Six Mile Run Reservoir

Round-trip: 4.3 miles
Elevation range: 40–80 feet
Difficulty: Easy
Hiking time: 2.25 hours
Best canine hiking season: Year-round
Regulations: Dogs must be leashed
Maps: USGS Monmouth Junction, NJ quadrangle; NJDEP Delaware
& Raritan Canal State Park
Information: Delaware & Raritan Canal State Park, (732) 873-3050,
www.njparksandforests.org; Delaware & Raritan Canal Commission,
www.dandrcanal.com

Getting there: Take Interstate 287 to exit 12 (Manville) and turn left
onto Route 623 for 3.2 miles. Turn left at the traffic light onto Weston
Canal Road (County Route 533 South) for 1.7 miles, then bear left onto
Millstone River Road (still County Route 533 South). Drive 2.6 miles
and turn left onto Blackwells Mills Road. At the stop sign, turn right
onto Canal Road. The park office and parking lot are on the left. Stop
in for a map.

This hike combines the Yellow, Red, and half of the Blue Trails for a variety
of habitats and terrain that will keep your dog interested and having fun.

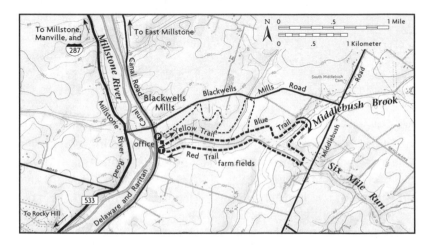

Furley checks out the sights and scents in a tall grass field.

The trail runs close to Six Mile Run, a wide, shallow stream with easy access for your dog to have a quick dip in hot weather.

Walk around the building to the right to pick up the Yellow Trail and enter the woods. The trail turns left onto a mowed path through a meadow of tall grass, then enters the woods again, following the stream for most of its 0.9-mile length.

Come out of the woods to a T intersection at a farm field and turn right onto the Blue trail. The path ambles beside sunny fields, occasionally dipping into the woods for shady respite. Half the land on this 3037-acre Six Mile Run Reservoir Site is leased to farmers. The rest is open fields, forest, and wetlands managed by the park until the time it is needed as a reservoir.

The trail rises slightly above a lowland inhabited by eastern red cedar. Turn right on a slight downhill and cross the lowland through tall grasses and rushes, then head into the woods and across the stream. Pass through an aging red cedar forest and eventually reach an exciting stream crossing. Just after a hard rain, the large stepping-stones may be inundated. Either wade across upstream of the stones where the water is about a foot deep or turn around. But, guaranteed, your dog will enjoy crossing the stream—and so will you.

Habitats and terrain change quickly on this path, from upland forest of different-aged red cedar stands, to groves of black walnut underlain with a carpet of grass and a stand of young maple saplings. Once on the Red Trail, always keep the farm fields on your left and the woods on your right on the way down again to the stream. At the road, make a right back to the parking lot. This is a fun hike for your dog.

31. Palisades: Alpine Loop

Round-trip: 8 miles
Elevation range: 10–500 feet
Difficulty: Moderate
Hiking time: 6 hours
Best canine hiking season: Spring, summer, fall
Regulations: Dogs must be leashed
Maps: USGS Yonkers, NY quadrangle; Palisades Interstate Park, New Jersey Section; NY-NJTC North Jersey Trails Maps 108 and 109
Information: Palisades Interstate Park Commission, (201) 768-1360, *www.njpalisades.org*

Getting there: From the north, on Palisades Interstate Parkway take exit 2 in Alpine. Turn right onto US Highway 9W, then right at the first light onto Alpine Approach Road. Bear right to the park headquarters on the left. From the south, take exit 2 and go straight to park headquarters on the left. It is 0.5 mile from exit 2 to the headquarters parking lot.

With a lot of sights, scents, sounds, and a varied terrain, this hike is dramatic and fun for you and your dog. Waterfalls, rivers of boulders

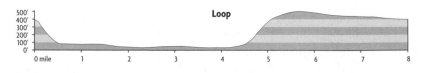

on hillsides, cliffs, birds of prey, old quarries, boulders to scramble over (if you like), lapping waves, woods, riverboats, skinny trails, wide paths, and a lot of human history make the hike interesting. Take a break on a big boulder anywhere.

Hike south along the road and turn left onto the orange-blazed Closter Dock Trail. The sign at the trailhead says "PATH TO RIVER." This rocky, wooded trail descends 460 easy feet to the white-blazed Shore Trail. Turn left onto the Shore Trail to hike north along the Hudson River, once known as the "New World Rhine."

At about 0.7 mile, just after a graceful waterfall sliding over boulders, the path splits. Both paths meet farther north, but stay to the right along

The Women's Federation Monument honors the members of the New Jersey State Federation of Women's Clubs who led the fight to save the Palisades from development.

Views from the Long Path across the Hudson River to New York are spectacular.

the water. Soon, an unusual "living room" and "kitchen" appear—tables with seats, a sofa, and a giant grill carved from boulders. In the 1800s, people on day excursions enjoyed the Excelsior Picnic Area. Now, let your canine pal take a water break as he listens to the sound of lapping waves against the river wall.

The trail rises above the water, through forest with occasional rivers of boulders that tumbled from the cliffs. Ospreys swoop from the highest trees down over the Hudson, some carrying dinner. Close to the river, Bowser will get some good scents. Look up to the left and see the famous Palisades cliffs of volcanic basalt.

On through an old garden of roses, the Shore Trail meets the blue-and-white-blazed Forest View Trail, which leaves to the left. You will take this, but first visit the Giant Stairs, a mile-long talus slope of Palisades diabase on the Shore Trail. Take a quick trip to see it and let Bowser get a taste of scrambling big rocks. It is 0.4 mile from the blue and white blazes to the Giant Stairs. On the way there, the path goes through a wild place that, until World War II, was a picnic area and ball field accessed only by hiking or boat. Your dog will like hiking through this sunny glade covered in vines.

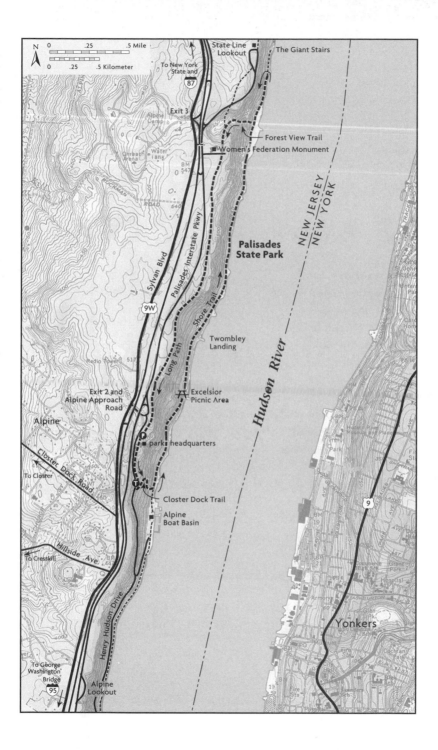

State Line
Lookout

The Giant Stairs

To New York
State and
87

Exit 3

Forest View Trail

Women's Federation Monument

NEW JERSEY
NEW YORK

Palisades
State Park

Sylvan Blvd

Palisades Interstate Pkwy

9W

Shore Trail

Long Path

Twombley
Landing

Hudson River

Radio Tower

Excelsior
Picnic Area

Exit 2 and
Alpine Approach
Road

Alpine

park headquarters

Closter Dock Road

To Closter

Closter Dock Trail

Alpine
Boat Basin

9

Hillside Ave.

To Cresskill

Henry Hudson Drive

Yonkers

To George
Washington
Bridge
95

Alpine
Lookout

Check out the talus, then return and follow the blue and white blazes up to the Long Path. For 520 feet, the trail shimmies along the hillside on switchbacks next to drop-offs and ambles up stone steps.

At the aqua-blazed Long Path, turn left and head south. At 0.2 mile, reach the Women's Federation Monument, built like a watchtower. Bring Bowser to the top of it for a treat. From gravel road to footpath, the trail traverses streams, woods, lands of former grand estates now gone wild, and side paths to great river views. The path takes you back to the parking lot.

32. Palisades: Englewood Loop

Round-trip: 8.7 miles
Elevation range: 10–430 feet
Difficulty: Moderate, with a difficult climb
Hiking time: 5 hours
Best canine hiking season: Fall, winter, spring
Regulations: Dogs must be leashed; parking fee from Memorial Day
   weekend through Labor Day
Maps: USGS Yonkers, NY quadrangle; Palisades Interstate Park New
   Jersey Section; NY-NJTC Hudson Palisades Trails Map 108
Information: Palisades Interstate Park Commission, (201) 768-1360,
   www.njpalisades.org

Getting there: From the north, on Palisades Interstate Parkway take exit 1 in Englewood Cliffs. Turn left toward the river to the Englewood Boat Basin. Drive beyond the marina and park in the second lot where the famous cliffs tower above you.

This hike rambles on beach, rocks, and boulders, past short rises and old docks, under trees, and over streams, always with the smell of the sea and the sound of lapping waves. It is a fun steeplechase path for experienced human and canine hikers only. Goldfinches and herons spy the autumn

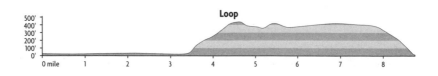

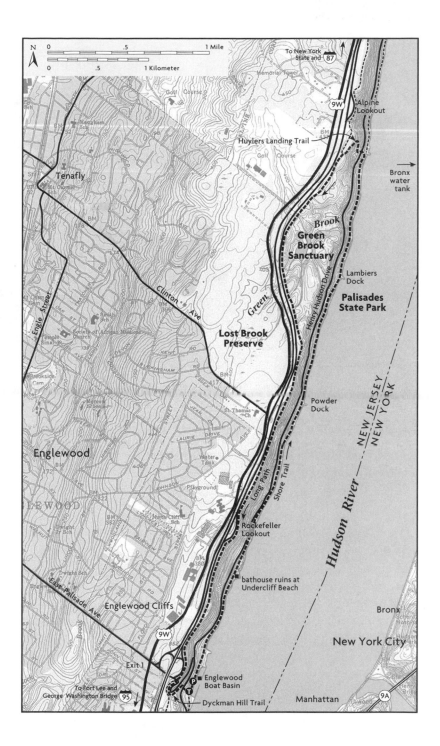

To New York State and 87

N
0   .5   1 Mile
0   .5   1 Kilometer

Memorial Tower

Golf Course

450

9W
Alpine Lookout

Huylers Landing Trail

Tenafly

Golf Course

Bronx water tank

Meacham

Brook

Green Brook Sanctuary

Clinton   Ave

Green

Lost Brook Preserve

Lambiers Dock

Palisades State Park

Henry Hudson Drive

Society of African National Church

Temple Sinai

Brookside Cem

St. Thomas Ch

Powder Dock

NEW JERSEY
NEW YORK

Englewood

Water Tank

Playground

Long Path

Shore Trail

ENGLEWOOD

Hudson River

North Cliffs Sch

Rockefeller Lookout

bathouse ruins at Undercliff Beach

Englewood Cliffs

Bronx

New York City

East Palisade Ave

9W

Exit 1

To Fort Lee and George Washington Bridge   95

P
T

Englewood Boat Basin

Dyckman Hill Trail

Manhattan

9A

The Long Path at Clinton Point affords a great view across the Hudson River to the Bronx. Lance enjoys the perspective.

hiker, while in summer, osprey hunt from cliffs to the river.

Pick up the white-blazed, north–south Shore Trail adjacent to the parking lot and head north 3.4 miles to the Huylers Landing Trail. The path runs close to the Hudson River shoreline but moves inland during high tide. Arrows point the way to the high-tide trail. It passes the ruins of a small bathhouse and, in about 30 minutes at about 0.7 mile, the stone foundations of a 1922 bathhouse at Undercliff Beach. Greenbrook Falls spills from a viaduct, bringing cool air temperatures as you boulder-hop across. The trail here is passable except, maybe, briefly after a very heavy rain. In that case, make your way up to the road, then back down after you cross over the falls.

Soon the red-blazed Huylers Landing Trail appears to the left across from the water tower in the Bronx. Turn left onto a steep woods road up to the macadam road. Sit on a boulder for a nice water break. Turn left on the road, then right, uphill into woods on wooden steps. At the top, turn left onto the aqua-blazed Long Path, heading south for 3.6 miles to the yellow Dyckman Hill Trail.

For about a mile, the trail undulates between Greenbrook Sanctuary and the parkway. After that, the trail turns away from the road and gets close to the cliffs around Clinton Point and Rockefeller Lookout for nice views of the Hudson River and New York. Keep a tight leash on your dog.

At the end of the woods, the trail reaches the corner of two roads. Walk down the steps to the road and around to your left on the sidewalk to pick up the yellow trail, which is basically a long stone stairway down a 340-foot drop on a hillside. If your dog is afraid of stairs, take the road down. The yellow trail follows the road a bit, then turns left down a multitude of steps, passing through a tunnel, over a stone path, and down more stone steps to the picnic area and your car.

33. Sourland Mountain Ridge Trail

Round-trip: 4 miles
Elevation range: 140–500 feet
Difficulty: Easy/moderate
Hiking time: 2.5 hours
Best canine hiking season: Fall, winter, spring
Regulations: Dogs must be leashed; carry out dog waste
Maps: USGS Rocky Hill, NJ quadrangle; Somerset County Park Commission, Sourland Mountain Preserve
Information: Somerset County Park Commission, (908) 722-1200, *www.somersetcountyparks.org*

Getting there: From US Highway 206 in Belle Mead, turn right onto County Route 601. Turn right onto East Mountain Road. At 1.1 mile, turn left into Sourland Mountain Preserve where, appropriately, two large boulders flank a gravel road.

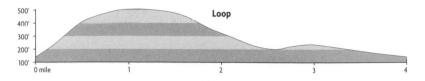

Sourland Mountain is a 10-mile-long volcanic ridge in the central New Jersey lowland. The 2780-acre preserve offers you and your dog a hike through quiet woods with different habitats, wildlife, an easy trail to follow, dramatic boulders, and a fun stream. You can't get lost here.

Pick up a map at the kiosk, or call ahead to receive one by mail. Cross the field to the trailhead and enter the woods on the rectangle-blazed Ridge Trail. A river of glacial boulders decorates the wide trail and mountainside, as if they had rolled down like marbles. In summer, hear the

A wide boardwalk makes for a pleasurable hike through a wet forest on Sourland Mountain.

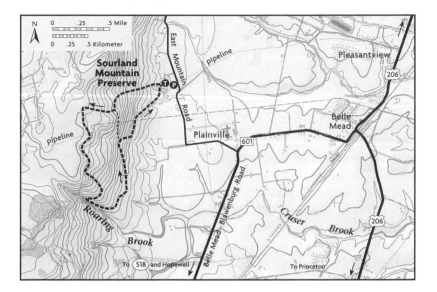

sound of cicadas among the tall American beech, oak, and tulip poplar. Spicebush scents the air on humid days.

Turn left at the wooden sign with trail markers over a boardwalk, then turn left. Go right at post 1, traveling steadily uphill over roots and rocks. The trail bends left at post 4 to head downhill. In about 30 feet, the trail splits. Bear left and look ahead for the blaze.

The crackle of paws and boots may stir some interesting birds in these quiet woods. Large birds of prey flit low through the trees. Some have a raucous call, providing interest for your dog.

The path runs close to a rocky stream, then onto a sunny gas pipeline, blooming in early fall with goldenrod, asters, and cattail. Take a quick side trip here to a small knoll to see across Somerset County all the way to New York on a clear day. Your dog will enjoy the breeze.

Into the woods, the trail follows a few switchbacks across the rocky stream. It's fun to watch your dog find the trail. A boardwalk carries you through an open wet forest with a ground cover of bright green grass, then turns left down a steep, rocky path armed with a hand rail, one of the park's many accoutrements built by Eagle Scouts.

The path continues to surprise—now a thin, soft, level footpath through young trees and shrubs, next through a stand of old junipers, then circling back to the boulders and spicebush. The trail makes a sharp, backward right at post 10, where it joins the triangle-blazed trail.

Cross the pipeline, wind through the woods, cross a field, and end at the pond next to the parking lot.

34. Watchung Reservation: Green Brook Loop

Round-trip: 6 miles
Elevation range: 160–440 feet
Difficulty: Moderate
Hiking time: 3.5 hours
Best canine hiking season: Year-round
Regulations: Dogs must be leashed
Maps: USGS Chatham, NJ quadrangle; Union County Board of
   Chosen Freeholders, Watchung Reservation
Information: Watchung Reservation, (908) 789-3670,
   www.unioncountynj.org/svcsgov/parksrec/trailsde.htm

Getting there: From Interstate 78 East, take exit 44. Turn left at the traffic light onto Glenside Avenue (County Route 527) at the bottom of the exit ramp. At 0.4 mile, turn right into the Deserted Village of Feltville parking lot.

The 2065-acre Watchung Reservation has 13 miles of blazed trails, 26 miles of bridle trails, and more than 40 miles of unmarked trails—plenty of space for you and Bowser to explore. With many access points, the white-blazed Sierra Trail has a lot of company—wild and tame. If your dog is well behaved on a leash, you both will enjoy the excursion.

Hike down the paved Cataract Hollow Road through the Deserted Village of Feltville, an 1840s mill town. The road through the village is the white-blazed Sierra Trail, which becomes a dirt bridle trail as it enters the woods after Masker's Barn, the last historic building. It runs through sun-dappled woods, heavy in birch and American beech trees. At a fork in the trail, go straight ahead, crossing several seeps on a narrow footpath

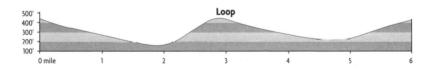

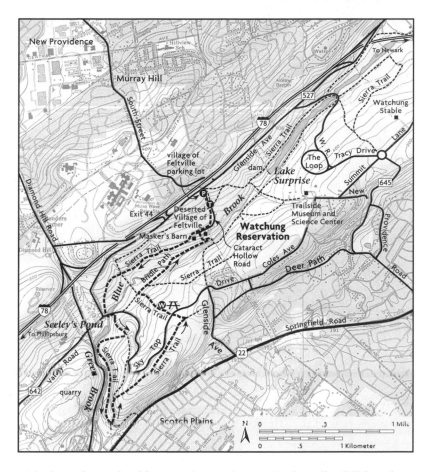

with close, dense shrubbery and enough sounds of small wildlife to keep your dog busy.

Come out of the woods into a clearing on the corner of Glenside Avenue and County Route 642 (Valley Road to the left and Sky Top Drive to the right). Go to your left and cross Sky Top Drive. Cross the bridge over Seeley's Pond and turn right onto the Sierra Trail just beyond the parking lot.

After a lot of ups and downs through open woods, the trail reaches an outcrop of chunky volcanic basalt that supports the same chestnut oaks of the conglomerate Kittatinny Ridge and the puddingstone ridges of the Highlands. This is a good spot for a drink, and Bowser will enjoy the breeze.

Let even more fun begin on the hike down past remnants of historic

The double-duty general store with second-floor church is one of the twentieth-century buildings in the Deserted Village of Feltville.

mill days to Green Brook, a deliciously feisty stream and a great spot for you and your dog to get your paws wet. This stream is the highlight of the trail. Hiking now through more ruins alongside an escarpment, the trail turns uphill. Watch for blazes to turn left.

Cross Sky Top Drive again and shortly arrive at a picnic area with a water fountain. Continue into the woods, down through an interesting pine and spruce plantation. In 0.3 mile, the trail turns right onto a bridle path. Soon the white blazes turn right uphill, but go straight, staying on the bridle path.

The path passes between the buildings of Feltville on the ridge on your left and Blue Brook on your right. Follow the trail as it bends uphill, rising toward Feltville and leaving Blue Brook behind. At the paved road turn right and follow it up to the parking lot.

35. Watchung Reservation: Lake Surprise Loop

Round-trip: 4 miles
Elevation range: 280–440 feet
Difficulty: Easy
Hiking time: 2.5 hours
Best canine hiking season: Year-round
Regulations: Dogs must be leashed
Maps: USGS Chatham and Roselle, NJ quadrangles; Union County Board of Chosen Freeholders, Watchung Reservation
Information: Watchung Reservation, (908) 789-3670, *www.unioncountynj.org/svcsgov/parksrec/trailsde.htm*

Getting there: From Interstate 78 East, take exit 44. Turn left at the traffic light onto Glenside Avenue (County Route 527) at the bottom of the exit ramp. At 0.4 mile, turn right into the Deserted Village of Feltville parking lot.

The white-blazed Sierra Trail meanders around the 2065-acre Watchung Reservation through various habitats and elevations. Because the park is crisscrossed with an intricate bridle path and trail system, the Sierra Trail pops up in places you least expect it. Lake Surprise is an easy walk in mostly shade with a lake for Bowser to cool off in. This is a popular place, perfect for a dog who enjoys meeting people and other dogs.

Take the paved road downhill to the white-square-blazed Sierra Trail, just after the equestrian sign. Turn left onto the trail into the woods. Starting as a wide bridle trail, it soon becomes a footpath bearing right, downhill. The trail zigzags, partly footpath, partly dirt road, until you reach Lake Surprise.

If you cross a stream before you see the lake, you have gotten off the

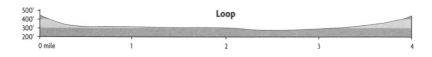

Farley and water lilies at narrow Lake Surprise

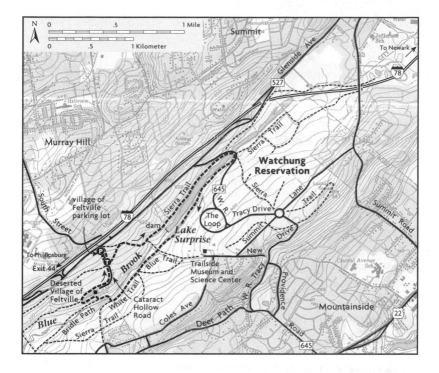

path; turn around and go back or just continue in this counterclockwise direction around Lake Surprise.

But continuing in a clockwise direction around the lake, the white blazes of the Sierra Trail closely follow the northern shoreline. In late August, sweet pepperbush scents the air.

At about 1.5 miles, the trail emerges onto County Route 645 and bears left across the road. Instead, stay close to the lake and hike along its southern side on an unmarked bridle trail under shady hemlock and grand rhododendron. This side of the lake is popular with people fishing and picnicking—some even playing with dogs. It offers easy access for Bowser to take a quick swim on leash.

Check out the dam, almost 1 mile from the road. About 500 feet past the dam, pick up the Blue Trail, crossing two boardwalks and leading to Blue Brook in a shady ravine. The Blue Trail turns left up along the ravine, but continue straight ahead onto the white Sierra Trail for only a few feet before it veers left uphill, then continue straight on an unmarked path that crosses the brook within 500 feet.

Go straight uphill as far as you can for about 200 feet and turn left onto a dirt bridle trail. See the buildings of the Deserted Village of Feltville as you wind your way up toward them. Turn right onto the paved road, which is also the Sierra Trail, and follow it uphill back to the parking lot. People live in some houses in Feltville, a historic 1840s mill town on the National Register of Historic Places. Please respect their privacy.

36. Garret Mountain Reservation Loop

Round-trip: 3.8 miles
Elevation range: 340–520 feet
Difficulty: Easy
Hiking time: 2.5 hours
Best canine hiking season: Fall, winter, spring
Regulations: Dogs must be leashed
Maps: USGS Paterson, NJ quadrangle
Information: Passaic County Parks Department, (973) 881-4832,
   www.passaiccountynj.org

Getting there: From Interstate 80 East, take exit 53 onto US Highway 46 East. Drive 3.9 miles to the exit for Valley Road North. At 6.1 miles, turn left onto Mountain Park Road. At 6.5 miles, turn right into the park entrance. The parking lot is 0.5 mile on the left, across the road from a stone observation tower.

Garret Mountain Reservation is located on the northernmost tip of First Watchung Mountain. You and your dog can stand on its volcanic cliffs with exciting views of the surrounding wall-to-wall suburbia of North Jersey and all its accoutrements. Basalt outcrops, small undulating hills, streams, and woods make this a fun hike for your canine pal. Expect to meet other dogs. Popular year-round, it is perhaps best to avoid the summer crowds.

   Cross the road and head up to the tower and bear left. The tower was built by silk tycoon Catholina Lambert after he built Lambert Castle, his

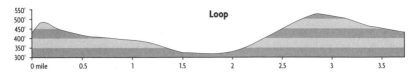

Debby and Brandy hike the Garret Mountain Trail around Barbour's Pond.

home on the cliff side below, in 1892. Both are on the state and national historic registers.

Two yellow-blazed paths of the Garret Mountain Trail appear—take the one left of the wall. The path traverses a ridge with wide, up-close views of Paterson and Clifton that extend to Manhattan. A quick side trip anytime to the edge of the cliff is worth it.

The footpath becomes wide and gravelly, crossing a parking lot, field, car vista, and road. Watch for blazes on guardrails and turn right uphill toward a radio tower. Cross the parking lot and turn left. Check out a tower remnant on a basalt outcrop to the left. Nose to the ground and shrubs, your dog will sniff lingering scents galore of dogs who have come here before.

The path leads down into woods away from the road. It meets the White Trail and seems to disappear. At this writing, some yellow blazes have been vandalized and erased. If still so, turn left to follow the white and head up over a few little rocky hillocks until you see a yellow blaze on a downhill switchback. Keep the road on your left in your line of mental vision, for the trail runs between the road and the cliff.

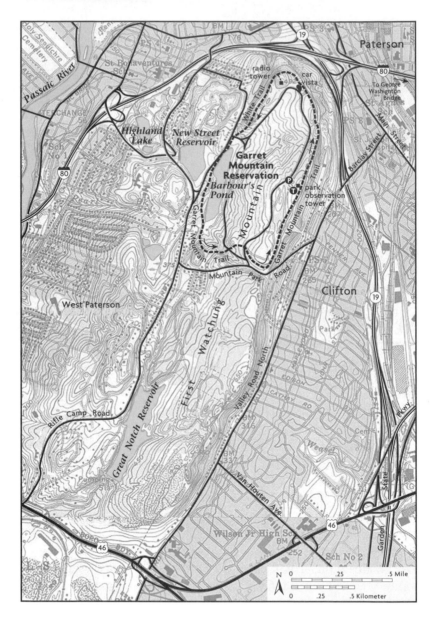

The trail crosses the street, then turns right and through a guardrail onto a greenway. Turn left at the end of Barbour's Pond into the woods. After crossing a stream, a trail shoots to the left, but go straight along a stream, then left uphill on a footpath.

Arrive at a yellow junction. Turn left (straight takes you to Rifle Camp Park). After crossing two roads, including the one you came in on, walk on the grass between road and outcrop outside of the park and watch for yellow blazes on trees. The path takes you up on a ridge and back to the tower.

This is a fun and easily accessible hike with interesting views and terrain. Wear sturdy boots for this hike over outcrops of chunky basalt.

37. Hoffman Park

Round-trip: 2.3 miles
Elevation range: 400–520 feet
Difficulty: Easy
Hiking time: 1.5 hours
Best canine hiking season: Year-round
Regulations: Dogs must be leashed
Maps: USGS High Bridge, NJ quadrangle; Department of Parks and
    Recreation, Hoffman Park
Information: Hunterdon County Department of Parks and
    Recreation, (908) 782-1158, *www.co.hunterdon.nj.us*

Getting there: From Interstate 78 in Lebanon, take exit 11 toward Pattenburg. At 1.3 miles, just after railroad tracks, turn left onto Main Street. Drive 2.7 miles to the end and turn right onto Baptist Church Road. The entrance to Hoffman Park is on the left.

Tranquility and peace describe this hike. A civility resides on this 354-acre former farm, whose mark on the land shows harmony between human and nature. Most of the paths here are roads—macadam, dirt, and grass.

Walk past the kiosk, through the gate, and turn left onto Hairpin Lane, a paved, steep switchback down through grassland managed for birds, with hedgerows and bird boxes, vernal pools, and ponds. American kestrels, northern harriers, eastern bluebirds, ground-nesting bobolinks,

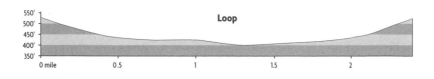

and eastern meadowlarks frequent these habitats, so keep your canine buddy especially close through the meadows. To the northeast, there are great views of the Highlands mountains.

At Manny's Pond, go straight onto Heron Road, a wide dirt road under trees set so far back it's like a grand boulevard in the woods. The land's heritage as farmland reveals itself. Turn left on the third path, Birch Way, and come out of the woods into meadow. Bird boxes and occasional red cedars accent the meadows.

Turn left onto Lehigh Lane, perhaps named for the railroad that chugs along the park's parallel boundary. Take a brief right onto Tunnel Road and check out a small pond, one of twenty-five, and a creek that runs through the railroad's tunnel.

Back on Lehigh, soon turn left onto Powerline Road, then right onto Middle Lane on a slight uphill. Turn left onto paved Manny's Pond Road with its fishing hole on the left. Uphill to the right is the great meadow you first came down.

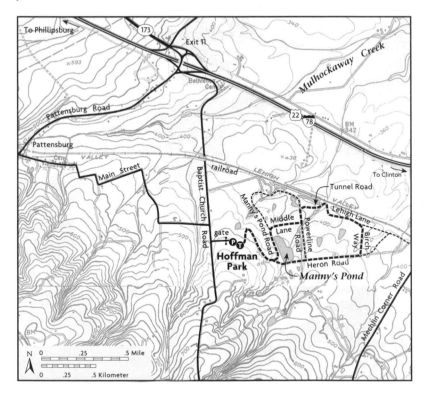

Hairpin Lane switchbacks through grassland managed for raptors and songbirds, with views of Highlands mountains.

These gentle paths, built long ago, provide an easy, open pace for your dog and a peace of mind that welcomes you to this land's past. For a longer hike in this wonderful park, check out all the interconnected roads. Wear blaze orange in fall.

38. Mountain Lakes Nature Preserve

Round-trip: 3.2 miles
Elevation range: 100–280 feet
Difficulty: Easy
Hiking time: 1.5 hours
Best canine hiking season: Year-round
Regulations: Dogs must be leashed
Maps: USGS Princeton, NJ quadrangle; New Jersey Trails Association
Information: Princeton Township, (609) 924-8720, *www.princetontwp. org*; Friends of Princeton Open Space, (609) 921-2772, *www.fopos.org*; New Jersey Trails Association, *www.njtrails.org*

Getting there: From the junction of US Highway 206 and County Route 27 (Nassau Street) in Princeton, take Route 206 North. At 0.7 mile, take

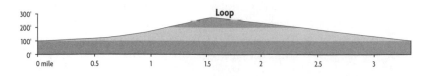

the jughandle at the light, crossing Route 206 onto Mountain Avenue. The Community Park North parking lot is 0.1 mile on the right.

This fast hike offers human and canine a fun few hours any time of year, especially in winter. The preserve is divided into three main areas, each with a distinctive adventure and blaze color of its own. This 400-acre park, once an estate, is a hidden jewel in the middle of suburbia, but you and your dog will soon feel far away and hear only birdsong. Your dog will keep cool meandering through wetlands and streams, a boulder field, and pine and spruce groves with a few large, interesting trees.

Pick up the blue-blazed Mountain Lakes Trail to the left of the parking lot. Be aware that this park is not blazed in the standard fashion. Instead, every trail in this section of the park is blazed blue so that hikers know generally where they are. The blacktop path soon becomes a soft, and sometimes quite wet, footpath that runs through surprisingly quiet, open deciduous woods. At the T, the trail turns right, heading downhill above a stream. At the end of a boundary fence, cross a wide grassy road. To the left, see remnants of an early 1900s commercial ice business: moss-covered icehouse foundations and, a little farther on, farm fields that produced straw for the buildings' insulation.

Bear left over a bridge at the Y and stay along the stream, then hike up a short rise to a lake human-made to produce the business's ice. Go left over the dam and stone-lined stream and right onto a wide path that rises above the lake. It must be fragrant here in early summer when the abundance of honeysuckle is in bloom. Continue straight past the falls, ignoring a blue trail that turns right.

Go through an opening in the fence, then turn right, hiking along the edge of a private farm field. Cross a pipeline, and in about 20 feet turn right onto a yellow-blazed trail that leads into the John Witherspoon Woods section of the park, where all trails are yellow.

Cross a stream on rock slabs and head uphill under birch, cedar, and a grand American beech. The trail splits at a giant, double-trunked red oak with a yellow blaze. Yellow blazes abound here, but turn left and hike along the stream. The trail soon crosses a rivulet and the stream.

Pass a sign for the Loop Trail, following the blazes toward houses on the outskirt of the park. The path weaves through a boulder field, beautiful in winter with silvery beech bark, lichens, moss, and evergreen ferns on rock, and patches of snow under sunlit deciduous woods. Pass a massive blazed tulip poplar.

Reach a junction of yellow blazes. Turn left onto a single-blazed trail and then right back to where the loop began. Turn left at the Y, cross the stream, and then find the trail headed right along a dry stream. This hike does not match the park map, which does not show all paths.

At a junction with a sign for Mountain Lakes House and John With-

A lichen-covered boulder field on a yellow-blazed trail

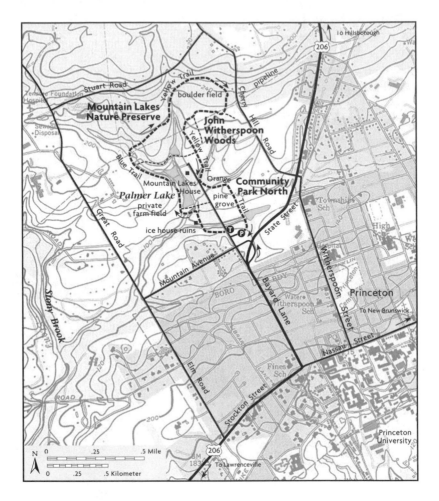

erspoon Woods, turn right downhill through a pine and spruce grove. Soon a sign pointing to the trailhead and parking lot signals that you are not lost, so take a quick walk to the right for a peek at Mountain Lakes House.

Back into the woods, turn right on the orange trail, unblazed here. You and Fido are now in the Community Park North section, where all trails are orange. The path clambers over a stream—ignore the occasional blue blaze. Turn right on another orange trail that crosses a pine grove. Go straight across a wide swath with orange blazes left and right, an unmarked woods road, and a small bridge, and follow the paved path back to your car.

39. Round Valley Loop

Round-trip: 2.5 miles
Elevation range: 400–520 feet
Difficulty: Easy
Hiking time: 1.5 hours
Best canine hiking season: Fall, winter, spring
Regulations: Dogs must be leashed; parking fee from Memorial Day weekend through Labor Day
Maps: USGS Flemington, NJ quadrangle; NJDEP, Round Valley Recreation Area
Information: Round Valley Recreation Area, (908) 236-6355, *www.njparksandforests.org*

Getting there: From State Route 22 West in Lebanon, take the jughandle across the highway onto Round Valley Access Road at a traffic light. Drive 1.4 miles and turn left into the park entrance. At 0.2 mile, turn right and drive to the second parking lot on the right.

The reservoir is home to mallards and other waterfowl.

This trail offers human and dog a very accessible and easy walk along the edge of a reservoir and a pretty hike through a pine plantation on a wide grassy path. The 4003-acre Round Valley Reservoir sits in the bowl of Cushetunk Mountain, formed by underground volcanic magma. At 180 feet deep, it can hold 55 billion gallons of water. The trails are pleasantly popular, even in winter, with other human and canine hikers and a few fishermen, but it is best to avoid the crowds from Memorial Day through Labor Day. With autumn's changing leaves and cooler days through the awakening of spring peepers, a peaceful walk can be yours and your dog's. This is a "no-excuses" central New Jersey hike.

Pick up the blue-blazed Water Trail that ambles along to the reservoir's edge. Hike the shoreline if you like, scrambling over rock, sand, moss, and plant debris. Make sure your dog's pads are tough enough to do this; otherwise, watch for blazes on a path that parallels the shore. At times when the reservoir is filled to capacity and the shoreline is underwater, you and Fido can hike along a parallel path.

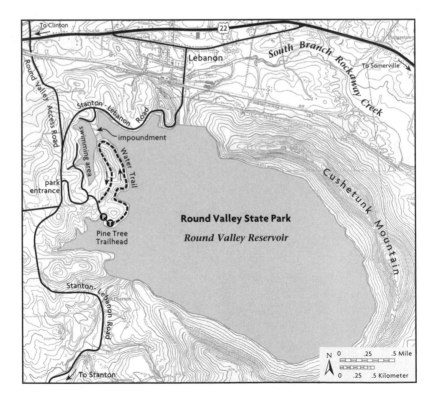

On the blue-blazed Water Trail, Lesley and pals hike down to the reservoir.

At about 0.7 mile, walk around the cove and follow the blue trail away from the water over little leaps and bounds. At 1.3 miles, turn left at the impoundment that separates the swimming area from the rest of the reservoir. The path uphill is short and somewhat steep through oak woods. Although this is a great hike for novice humans and dogs, take your time going to the top. The trail levels out, and the green Pine Tree Trailhead appears about 0.3 mile later. Either direction travels over a broad path with occasional traprock outcrops through pines, bringing you back to the road slightly above the parking lot.

40. Wickecheoke Creek Preserve

Round-trip: 3.4 miles
Elevation range: 80–200 feet
Difficulty: Easy
Hiking time: 2 hours
Best canine hiking season: Year-round
Regulations: Dogs must be leashed
Maps: USGS Stockton, NJ quadrangle
Information: New Jersey Conservation Foundation, (908) 234-1225, *www.njconservation.org*

Getting there: Take State Highway 29 North to just above Stockton. Turn left into the almost-hidden Delaware & Raritan Canal State Park parking lot, just before the historic stone and wood buildings of the Prallsville Mills and Visitor Center, or park in the Mills parking lot 0.1 mile above it.

If ever there were pristine woods in central New Jersey, this is it. Clean trails, sparkling trout-stocked waters, and a sense of sanctity prevail. You and your dog will enjoy this energetic creek and wide swaths of bedrock, the solitariness of the hike, and walking down an old-fashioned country road.

It takes a little bit of road hiking to get there, but it is well worth it. Walk left on State Highway 29, then right on County Route 519. After about 50 feet, watch for red blazes and hike along the creek.

The trail emerges on Lower Creek Road, a fun-to-walk, one-lane country road with almost no traffic, for a short distance. Just after an iron guardrail, the trail heads back into woods and runs beside the creek that rushes westward to the Delaware River. It veers around bends and fern- and moss-covered rock walls. Hemlock trees line one side of the creek, hardwoods the other. The water rushes over rocks and quiets out in gentle places. A male mallard sits on a rock, while a female glides out into the water.

Onto the road again, turn right and walk over the iron bridge. Continue down the road with the creek now on your left. Watch for the red blazes on the left at an aluminum gate and a wood sign that says "DONALD & BEVERLY JONES FOOTPATH, 1.3 MILES TO PRALLSVILLE MILLS."

Hike into these magnificent woods. Go down to the creek where milky-white water rushes over rock chopped into blocks by nature. The path is wide, the stream pristine, on land that will transport you and your dog far away.

The streambed is wide and deep, lined with bedrock. When the Wickecheoke rages after a good rain must be the perfect time to see it. Six-foot-tall goldenrod covers a gravel-based island in the middle—surely spectacular in fall. Out on the road again, hike a little more until you see a freshet spilling from under the road into the stream, bounded by massive rhododendron that flounce down the slope. Head back the way you came.

Sounds of wildlife attract Tank as he explores Wickecheoke Creek.

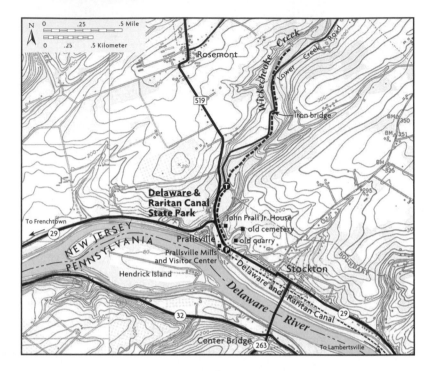

The Red Trail is a work in progress as the New Jersey Conservation Foundation procures the missing pieces of the land puzzle. So, before you leave, grab a snack for you and your dog and enjoy it on what will one day be the beginning of the Red Trail, now just a skinny ridge trail. Across State Highway 29 from the parking lot, go up the stone steps to the right of the John Prall Jr. House. Follow the red-blazed trail on a skinny path uphill above a ravine and a defunct quarry that was dug down to the water table, hence the pond. Continue up to a historic cemetery in the woods. This is the end of the trail at this point, but it's worth seeing. Go back the way you came.

THE SOUTHERN COASTAL PLAINS

From Sandy Hook to Cape May, the South Jersey coastline extends 125 miles over mainland, barrier island, spit, and hook. Drowned again and again by ancient seas, the land was built up by sediments deposited and washed away. About 100 million years ago, sandy deposits began to form first the Inner Coastal Plain, and then the Outer Coastal Plain. Then glacial sands and gravels washed down to the Coastal Plains as waves sculpted the shoreline.

A line of hills, from 100 to almost 400 feet high, separates the Inner and Outer Coastal Plains. These "cuestas" are capped with cemented sands and gravel, making them less resistant to erosion than the surrounding loose sands and gravels of the plains. Soils of the Inner Coastal Plain are more fertile and conducive to richer plant growth, resulting in more diverse forests. Soils of the Outer Coastal Plain are sandier and hold little moisture or fertility for plants, especially in the Pine Barrens. In many places, the water table is at the surface, resulting in swamps and marshes.

For the human and canine hiker, this habitat variety enables a diversity of hikes. Human and dog can hike the 50-mile Batona Trail or the maze of dry, sandy roads of the Pine Barrens, a vast 1.4-million-acre wilderness, and the junglelike swamps of the Inner Coastal Plain. Experience the sand dunes on Sandy Hook and a hike on a barrier island, an offshore sand ridge that sits only slightly above high tide. Island Beach State Park is one of the last as the islands move toward the mainland at an average rate of 2 feet per year.

Hike in the cool weather, after a heavy frost, or do your canine hiking buddy a favor—talk to your veterinarian about a killed Lyme disease vaccine—and hike in the warmth of the summer.

Hike these places. You and your dog will be glad you did.

41. Island Beach

Round-trip: 3.4 miles
Elevation range: Sea level
Difficulty: Easy
Hiking time: 2 hours
Best canine hiking season: Fall, winter, spring
Regulations: Dogs must be on 6-foot leash; day fee
Maps: USGS Barnegat Light, NJ quadrangle; NJDEP, Island Beach
State Park
Information: Island Beach State Park, (732) 793-0506,
www.njparksandforests.org

Getting there: Take the Garden State Parkway (I-87) to exit 82 (State Route 37 East) to the island. Turn right onto State Route 35 South to the park entrance. One road bisects the 10-mile-long park, whose approximate 1-mile width shifts with the tide. The road separates the oceanside primary and secondary dunes and thickets from the maritime forest, freshwater wetlands, tidal marshes, and bayshore habitats. Follow the road 8.2 miles to the last parking lot, 23, and head to the beach.

This barrier island park offers you and your dog an off-season stroll on the beach minus the crowds, a close-up view of Barnegat Inlet, a glimpse of coastal habitats, and a healthy dose of salt air. There is plenty to keep your dog interested—crashing waves, squawking gulls, diving seabirds, surf anglers, and seaside scents for a different kind of sniffing. A quick side trip on a boardwalk to the bay offers a hiking canine the new experience of standing on a platform over big water.

Dogs are permitted year-round in the area south of bathing unit 2, and in the ocean swimming areas from the day after Labor Day to the Friday before Memorial Day weekend. They are not allowed on bird-blind trails.

The 1.5-mile stretch of shore from the parking lot to Barnegat Inlet curves along the park's Southern Natural Area, a wildlife sanctuary. It

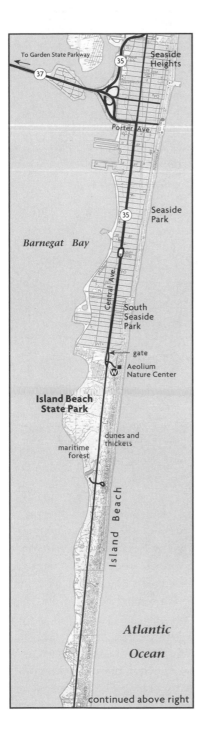

To Garden State Parkway

35

37

Seaside
Heights

Porter Ave.

35

Seaside
Park

Barnegat   Bay

Central Ave.

South
Seaside
Park

gate

W Aeolium
Nature Center

**Island Beach
State Park**

dunes and
thickets

maritime
forest

Island Beach

Atlantic

Ocean

continued above right

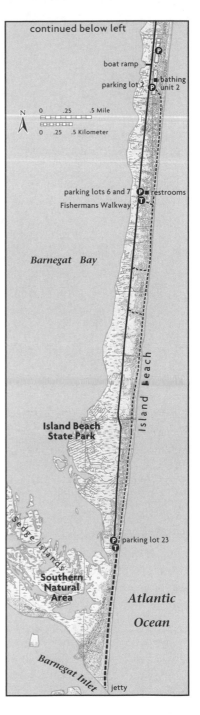

continued below left

P

boat ramp

parking lot 2   P   bathing
unit 2

N

0   .25   .5 Mile

0   .25   .5 Kilometer

parking lots 6 and 7   P   restrooms
T
Fishermans Walkway

Barnegat   Bay

Island Beach

**Island Beach
State Park**

Sedge Islands

**Southern
Natural
Area**

P   parking lot 23
T

Atlantic

Ocean

Barnegat Inlet

jetty

Little One crosses the dunes on Fisherman's Walkway.

is new land formed over the last century by long shore currents that dropped sand here from the shore farther north. The beach is busy with surf anglers and their vehicles. If you are lucky, you might see a gull swallowing its catch. Commercial fishing ships ride the horizon and float through the inlet. Hiking the beach in warm weather offers the perfect opportunity to take a swim with your pal in the sea.

The tides uncover interesting things in the sand—parts of ships, timbers, shacks, and, once, even an old schooner. High tides combined with strong winds shape the sand into natural shelves called "scarps," some up to 15 feet tall. They disappear with other tides, so beware of drop-offs and your footing. Although your dog is leashed, keep a careful watch.

Soon the jetties of Barnegat Inlet come into view and the 1856 Barnegat Lighthouse peeks over the dunes. The jetties were reconstructed in the early 1990s to protect the lighthouse after the first ones washed away. Although the dunes here are the most stable in the park and support a well-sustained plant community, they are still being revamped as a result of the jetty construction.

Back in the car, head north again. Along the road, more paths and boardwalks lead from parking lots to the beach and bay, providing a choice of hikes of any length. A quick walk on the boardwalk at parking lot 6-7 offers more education for dog and human, with a glimpse at a cross-section of island habitats. This boardwalk is heavily used by handicapped people and groups, so keep your canine buddy on a tight leash.

Cross the road, and take the boardwalk to the bay through a thicket of wind and salt-shorn American holly, red and Atlantic white cedar, oak, magnolia, bayberry, and other bayshore plants. Go 0.1 mile to a deck overlooking the bay—fun for Fido. Return and take the boardwalk back to the ocean for 0.1 mile on Fishermans Walkway with Coastal Heritage interpretive signs explaining the habitats.

Beach heather mounds cover the dunes and bloom yellow around Memorial Day. *Rosa rugosa* blooms in June and carries its hips into the summer. Beach plums bloom in spring and fruit in September when the cranberries begin to ripen.

If you hop on the beach at lot 2, it is 5.8 miles to the jetty at Barnegat Inlet. An outdoor water faucet at the Aeolium Nature Center freezes in winter, so bring water for you and your dog. Winter wind can be brutal; bring a hat and scarf for you and a coat or windbreaker for your trusty dog.

42. Shark River Loop

Round-trip: 3.4 miles
Elevation range: Sea level–100 feet
Difficulty: Easy
Hiking time: 2 hours
Best canine hiking season: Fall, winter, spring
Regulations: Dogs must be leashed
Maps: USGS Asbury Park, NJ quadrangle; Monmouth County
    Park System

Information: Shark River Park, Monmouth County Park System, (732) 922-4080 or 3868, *www.monmouthcountyparks.com*

Getting there: Take the Garden State Parkway to exit 100 (State Route 33 East). Make a right at the first traffic light onto Schoolhouse Road. The park office and parking are 0.5 mile farther.

Hiking the Shark River Loop is a joy for human and dog. In winter, its gently rolling terrain offers solitude and shelter from the wind. Its open woods and sandy roads are pleasant and easy—even on the "challenging" trail. In all seasons, it is a birder's paradise. Your dog will love the scents and sounds and can take a dip in the Shark River to get cool. Saunter on a wide, flat sand road, a footpath over forested sand dunes, and riverside with a few short heart-pumpers up stairways. It is a great solo hike with your dog when no one else has the time to accompany you. Less than a mile from the Garden State Parkway, this is a "no-excuses" walk—so get out with your dog who will welcome the outing.

Stop in the shelter building and pick up a trail map. Then, cross

The Cedar Loop Extension slips through a tall stand of Atlantic white cedars.

Schoolhouse Road and enter the woods at the trailhead. It is unmarked right here, so stay to the left, paralleling the road over little hills and a stream. The immediate array of terrain, and the nearness of plants and birdsong stimulate the senses of you and your dog.

At a trail marker, follow the Hidden Creek Trail blazed with a blue square. Just beyond the sand road, pick up the black-diamond-blazed Rivers Edge Trail that takes you 0.75 mile along the bank of the Shark River, where your dog can wade in warm weather to cool off. The river

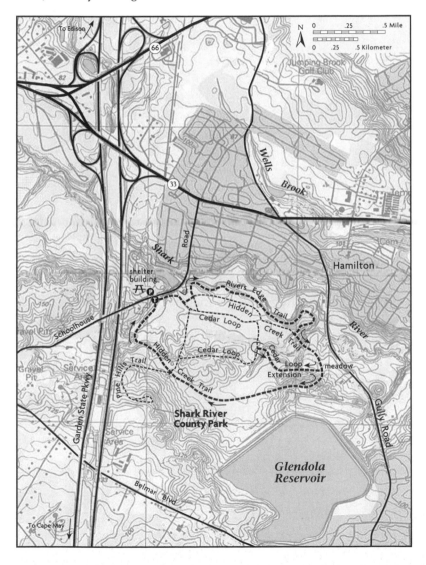

River's Edge Trail along the Shark River is an easy winter walk.

weaves through oak, sassafras, leucothoe, American holly, mountain laurel, musclewood, a lot of catbriar, and highbush blueberry. Because fire is not a management tool here, the pitch pine/scrub oak forest has become a mixed oak/hardwood forest due to natural succession.

The river is fast and narrow beside the scooped-out trail. It plays hide-and-seek with you and your dog, who must climb short, steep knolls—with a choice of stairs or path—to catch up to it again. For a little mental challenge and more fun for Fido, let him choose the way. At the top of the first climb, turn left onto the trail. There is no blaze ahead, but for reinforcement turn around and see the black diamond. As long as the trail runs beside the river, stay on it, as it eventually runs through floodplain.

The trails are marked just enough to leave a little to the adventurous imagination, and there are many unmarked side paths. Always remember, stay on the path you are on unless you see a blaze that you want.

At the top of a hill, turn left onto the blue-blazed Hidden Creek Trail that encircles the park. Here, the trail is a wide sand road where both of you can jog or stroll through sweet gum, pitch pine, grey birch, and maple. The quick-changing habitat here keeps Fido from being bored. The path crosses a meadow diagonally, but just before you get to the other side, take the green-circle-blazed Cedar Loop Extension to see the Atlantic white cedar trees, tall and protected with shaggy reddish bark. Or, do the whole circular Cedar Trail on the flats, for an extra 1.4 miles that will bring you right back to this spot. Go back to the meadow, a great place to see hawks, and turn right at the field and right again following blue blazes into the woods.

The path ambles on in many disguises—a cut in a moss-covered sand dune, dirt footpath, sand road—all gentle on your dog's legs and paws. The surprisingly hilly terrain is actually sand dunes formed by fierce winds during glacial times. The latest theory pinpoints this region as a semi-desert then. Side excursions lead to pine-covered lowlands and hills. Benches are strategically placed at streams where one may sit and contemplate these lovely coastal woods as your dog relaxes and takes a dip.

A trail marker at a sandy crossroads says the Hidden Creek Trail goes straight across. The Pine Hills Trail leads to the left for an extra 3 miles round-trip, while a right accesses the Cedar Trail. But walk straight ahead, under dense evergreen cover, over streams, and through phragmites on a boardwalk back to the car. This park offers a great introductory hike on hills for a novice dog.

43. Cheesequake Blue Trail Loop

Round-trip: 2.5 miles
Elevation range: 10–70 feet
Difficulty: Easy
Hiking time: 1.5 hours
Best canine hiking season: Fall, winter, spring
Regulations: Dogs must be leashed; entrance fee from Memorial Day weekend to Labor Day
Maps: USGS South Amboy, NJ quadrangle; NJDEP, Cheesequake State Park
Information: Cheesequake State Park, (732) 566-2161, *www.njparksandforests.org*

Getting there: Take the Garden State Parkway to exit 120. Turn right at the bottom of the exit and right again at the first traffic light at 0.2 mile. At the next light at 0.1 mile, turn right onto County Route 689 and go to a T intersection. Turn right onto Gordon Road and drive straight into the park. It is best not to worry about the names of the roads—they change by the quarter-mile. Pay an entrance fee at the booth and drive to the first parking lot on the left with all trailheads.

Salt meadow grass dominates the high part of the salt marsh on the Blue Trail. Wind and water whip it into "cowlicks."

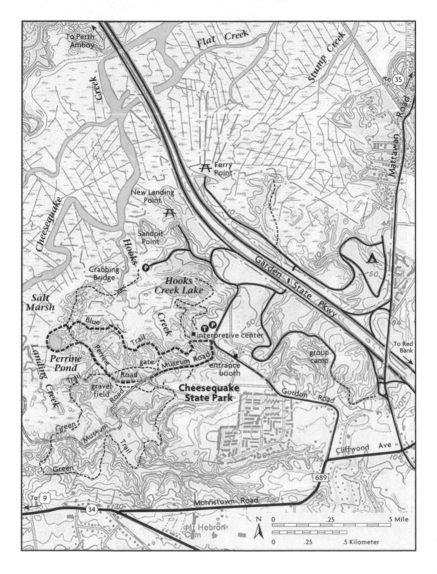

This soft trail meanders through tidewater salt marsh, encountering southern plant species such as spring and summer-blooming fragrant magnolias, a lot of birdsong for your dog to pick up his ears and listen to, and diverse terrain with different scents and sights. Canine and human feet will feel good pounding this sand. The path's gentle ups and downs are short and fun through the park's state-designated Natural Area. Bring plenty of water for your dog because the streams here are

Serenity on Perrine's Road heading to Museum Road

brackish—a mix of salt and fresh water. This is a "no-excuses" hike—just 1 mile off the parkway.

Cheesequake's trails are mostly civilized and close to the crowds. In fall and winter, they are popular places to walk the local dogs.

The Blue Trail starts at the trailhead for the Blue, Red, Green, and Yellow Trails as a sandy path with no rocks, a treat after climbing the dramatic northwestern hills of New Jersey. The Blue Trail shortly crosses a stream on a wooden footbridge, then heads uphill to the Interpretive Center in the woods complete with wildlife preserve, passing through red maple and blackjack oak with an understory of sweet pepperbush.

You might want to stop in the dog-friendly center where naturalists keep fresh water bowls and a well-stocked can of doggy treats for your hiking buddy. Large, up-to-date maps of the park's rerouted trails are posted both inside and outside in the kiosk. The center is open Wednesday through Sunday from 8:00 AM to 4:00 PM, and seven days during the summer.

Soon the Blue Trail climbs wooden stairs with open risers and turns right. It winds its way down to the open, sunny salt marsh, with a large pine guarding its edge. Take the boardwalk over Hook's Creek, through stands of cattail and groundsel tree, and continue up into the shady hills. The scent of salt and plants will tantalize your dog.

On a hilltop, the leathery black gum tree and fragrant bayberry of candle fame accompany the hiker and dog. Soon, the path winds out into the sun and turns right onto a short extension of sandy Perrine Road. Go about 30 feet and turn left at the fork to hike around Perrine Pond, a more-scenic reroute of the Blue Trail.

Pass the pond on the left and a salt marsh on the right in the park's Natural Area. The trail becomes a gravel road that slices through a field with bluebird and purple martin houses. It turns right onto the wide, dirt Perrine Road again, now under cooling, shady woods. At the gate, turn left and hike the dirt Museum Road back to the parking lot.

44. Hartshorne Woods: Grand Tour Trail

Round-trip: 3.5 miles
Elevation range: 80–240 feet
Difficulty: Moderate
Hiking time: 2.5 hours
Best canine hiking season: Year-round
Regulations: Dogs must be leashed
Maps: USGS Sandy Hook West, NJ quadrangle; Monmouth County
   Board of Recreation Commissioners, Hartshorne Woods Park
Information: Monmouth County Park System, (732) 842-4000,
   www.monmouthcountyparks.com

Getting there: Take the Garden State Parkway (I-87) to exit 117 to County Route 36 East. Turn right onto Navesink Avenue in Highlands at 11.9 miles. Drive 0.5 mile to the Buttermilk Valley parking lot on the left. All trailheads are here. The Monmouth County Park System likes visitors to gain as much adventure from their treks in the woods as possible; therefore, signs are kept to a minimum. This is a good thing, and you and Spike can't get lost anyway—the Atlantic Ocean is to the east.

The Grand Tour Trail is a dream on canine and human feet. The soft loam underfoot feels as if you are walking on air. Hartshorne Woods contains everything you need in a hike—gentle hills with dramatic vegetation, diverse habitats, up-close wildlife, which will keep Spike busy sniffing, and surprises along the way. It is a fun, made-to-order, no-excuses hike

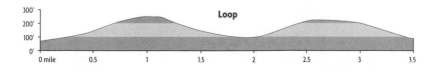

that will keep your dog happy and in shape. The park map calls the Grand Tour challenging, but if your dog is used to hiking the rocky northern trails, it is a breeze and a pleasure.

At the kiosk area, walk to the far left and head uphill on the blue-blazed Laurel Ridge Trail, here an unmarked dirt road. At 0.4 mile, turn left onto the black-diamond-blazed Grand Tour Trail. Climb to a hilltop through mountain laurel and oak. The trail curves back to the dirt road and heads downhill, crossing other dirt roads, including one with a log bench. Remember to always go straight unless a blaze tells you to turn, or if you are adventurous.

Towering tulip trees and spring-action paths in the mini hills and valleys of the Grand Tour Trail

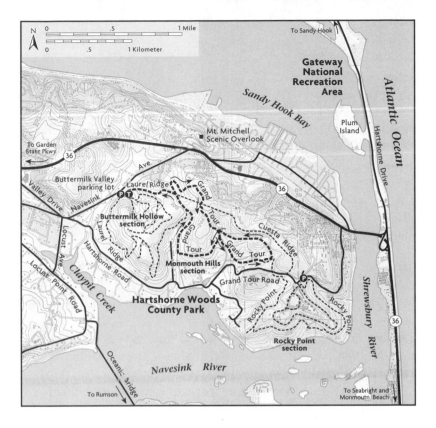

Courteous mountain bikers share this trail, which, in places, appears to zoom around stands of laurel on hillsides, banking in the turns. It is made for swiftness with moist, smooth soil. Toward the Monmouth Hills section of the park, the land is a series of miniature hills and valleys covered in towering tulip trees rising above laurel and blueberries. Sunlight streams through the canopy.

Look for a trail marker at the bottom of the hill to the right. Soon the trail leaves the woods and enters a magical-looking valley where everything is covered in vines—nature's topiaries. Go straight onto the skinny, sandy path. Follow it under tunnels of grapevine and into the woods again. Wildlife seems to like this area, where you'll see low-flying hawks, chipmunks, and large raucous birds. Patches of berry bushes shelter deer. Talk with your canine companion so as not to startle wildlife.

As the trail winds around to complete its easterly loop, there is snow fencing on the right. Go straight across and back from where you came.

Michelle, Dixie, and Angela enjoy the day on the Laurel Ridge Trail.

Turn right at the sawed-off tree stump with a wooden sign for the Laurel Ridge Trail. The parking lot is to the right.

As of this writing, some blazes need replacing. One of them signaled a left turn from the easterly loop to the westerly loop of the Grand Tour Trail at about 1 mile into the hike.

Hartshorne Woods is a series of fascinating miniature landscapes as one wanders the soft dirt path. Bring plenty of water with you on this hike, for the only available water is at the trailhead fountain to the right of the kiosk. Hold the faucet mechanism down till the water tumbles up from below the frost line. This walk in the woods will make Spike forget all about his couch potato life. He'll just sink into the joys of the trail.

45. Batsto Village Loop

Round-trip: 3 miles
Elevation range: 10–20 feet
Difficulty: Easy
Hiking time: 2 hours
Best canine hiking season: Late fall through June
Regulations: Dogs must be leashed
Maps: USGS Atsion, NJ quadrangle; NJDEP, Wharton State Forest
   Map C

Information: Wharton State Forest, (609) 561-0024,
www.njparksandforests.org

Getting there: From the Garden State Parkway South, take exit 52 (New Gretna). Turn left onto County Route 654 for 1 mile, then right onto US Highway 9 South for 1.5 miles. Turn right onto County Route 542 West for 12.5 miles, then right into the historic Batsto Village. The visitor center is on the left. From the Garden State Parkway North, take exit 50 (New Gretna) and turn left onto County Route 542 West and follow as above.

Wharton State Forest lies in the heart of the Pine Barrens. Its 114,000 acres encompass typical pineland habitat, long stretches of trails, three rivers, many streams, two Natural Areas, and all the hiking you and your dog could want among the pines. This hike, although relatively minute, takes you along a river, through oak–pine woods, over a great dam by a

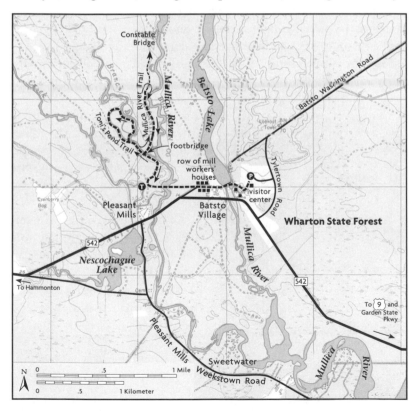

beautiful lake, and through a historic village. There is a lot for Fido to see in this popular end of the forest. Batsto began life in 1766 as both a bog iron and window glass company town, changing to agriculture and forest products in the late 1800s.

Walk past the visitor center toward Batsto Village, then turn right and go past the mansion. From the town's sidewalk to a sand road, hike across Batsto Lake on a plank bridge that allows all your dog's senses to be engaged. The outflow below the bridge races over the dam with a furious sight and sound, while just across the dam an 1882 sawmill stands on the far corner of this serene lake. The sand trail leads through a row of mill workers' houses from the early 1800s, lined with holly among other types of trees.

At the sandy cul-de-sac at forest's edge, a footpath to the orange-blazed Toni's Pond Trail and the yellow-blazed Mullica River Trail shoots diagonally to the right. Traveling into the woods of typical Pine Barrens species including blackjack oak and bayberry, the trail landscape seems like a fairyland in winter when snow still clings to branches. At a woodsy junction, the path jogs right, then left. Soon yellow turns right over the Sleeper Branch of the Mullica River, but go straight on orange. The path follows the Sleeper, sprinkled with islands of cedar and blueberry. This

trail is so energizing, you may start to jog down the path with your dog. Cross a footbridge, then zip around forest gaps with a few pines that look like someone's backyard, and along edges of dense swamp. At a T intersection, turn right over a bridge and head back.

At the yellow trail, turn left over a footbridge for a half-mile side trip upriver to the Mullica's banks. Turn around and head back. Cross the footbridge and turn left onto the orange and yellow trails back to the historic

Paths through the trees are made even more glorious in the snow, like the ones at Batsto Village.

village and your car. Your dog will enjoy the sociability of this trail and village.

For more hikes, numerous trails of varying lengths begin at the visitor center.

46. Cattus Island

Round-trip: 2.3 miles
Elevation range: 0–10 feet
Difficulty: Easy
Hiking time: 1 hour
Best canine hiking season: Late fall through June
Regulations: Dogs must be leashed; pick up after your dog; doggy bags provided
Maps: USGS Toms River, NJ quadrangle; Ocean County Parks and Recreation, Cattus Island County Park
Information: Cattus Island County Park, Cooper Environmental Center, (732) 270-6960, *www.oceancountyparks.org*

Getting there: From the Garden State Parkway, take exit 82 to State Route 37 East. Drive about 5 miles and take the jughandle, heading north, onto Fischer Boulevard. At the fourth traffic light, turn right onto Cattus Island Boulevard. Turn left into the park entrance. Parking is on the right.

This little hike, packed with interesting sights, offers human and dog a quick, easy walk into bayside habitats—upland forest, swamp, salt marsh, open woods, and a sandy beach. Wide paths help keep your dog out of tick habitat. The hike is open and sunny with a cheerful dose of nature, especially in winter. Cooper Environmental Center has freshwater spigots and wildlife exhibits.

From the environmental center, go right around the building to pick up the unblazed road that starts out as packed sand and becomes crushed shell. It takes you through a salt marsh with great close-up and distant views. Salt marshes comprise more than 70 percent of Cattus Island—an important fact since more than 75 percent of the salt marshes in Barnegat Bay has been developed.

To the right, see Lavalette across Barnegat Bay. On the mudflats, great blue and little blue herons feed in shallow tidal pools among smooth

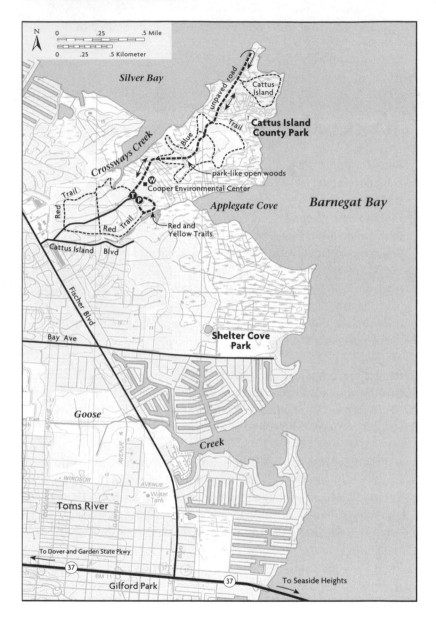

cordgrass. Go through an oak–pitch pine upland forest where persimmon trees grow among spring's heady bloomer, sweetbay magnolia.

Open parklike woodlands appear between wetlands. In the early 1900s, Cattus Island was purchased by the Cattus family of New York City for

A great blue heron searches for food in a tidal pool on the mudflats.

recreation. Sections of the land, in reality a peninsula, were cleared and these parklike areas remain. The open woods give way to the high salt marsh where ospreys return in March.

The path ends at the beach. You can walk along the edge and Fido can walk in the surf. New sounds and sights await him—gulls and ducks on water and the sound of lapping waves.

Go back to the environmental center the same way you came. If the winter cold has driven ticks away for the season, you may want to venture out to see a salt marsh up close by hiking a stretch of the Blue Trail on the right.

Back at the center, as you head toward the car, turn left onto the Red Trail boardwalk over a freshwater swamp. Atlantic white cedar filled this swamp until the 1950s when the Point Pleasant Canal opened, allowing an influx of saltwater that increased the salinity. Today, few white cedars remain. But it must be yummy here in summer when the blueberries and cranberries ripen and sweet pepperbush, sweetbay magnolia, and swamp azalea bloom.

47. Estell Manor Loop

Round-trip: 3.7 miles
Elevation range: 10–30 feet
Difficulty: Easy
Hiking time: 2.5 hours
Best canine hiking season: Late fall through June
Regulations: Dogs must be leashed
Maps: USGS Mays Landing, NJ quadrangle; Atlantic County Park
System, Estell Manor County Park
Information: Estell Manor Park, (609) 645-5960,
www.aclink.org/PARKS/mainpages/estell.asp

Getting there: From the Garden State Parkway, take exit 44 and turn right onto County Route 575 South. Turn right at the traffic light onto US Highway 30 West. Drive to Egg Harbor City, 10 miles from the Parkway, and turn left onto State Route 50 South, which turns left again 7.4 miles later. The park entrance is 3.5 miles ahead on the left.

A maze of sand roads, with names like TNT Road, crisscross the park, allowing for hikes of different lengths. For a good cross-section of Pine Barrens habitats, with minimum exposure to ticks, take a hike on the 1.8-mile boardwalk, circling back on a wide sand road. The United Nations has designated the Pine Barrens as an International Biosphere Preserve. More than 1 million acres are designated as the New Jersey Pinelands National Reserve, and most of that is protected by state legislation.

History abounds here, and an artesian well drilled in the early 1900s offers human and canine a safe, refreshing drink. This is a great place to spend the day. Bring lunch and a snack for Fluffy.

Behind the Warren E. Fox Nature Center, take the paved path to the 1.8-mile Swamp Trail on the left through upland forest and dense Atlantic white cedar swamp. Cement ruins of a World War I munitions manufacturing plant, known as Bethlehem Loading Company, and its company town, Belcoville, are scattered through the woods. It's hard to believe that 5000 people lived in this pine forest and swampland. All trails in the park are abandoned company railroad beds.

At a kiosk, bear right on the boardwalk. Trees diminish and the vegetation gets reedier. The landscape looks exotic. By this time, your dog

The ruins of a 1918 shell magazine of the Bethlehem Loading Company stands in the swamp at the end of the boardwalk. A spigot from an artesian well is located in front and is a great place for water for human and dog.

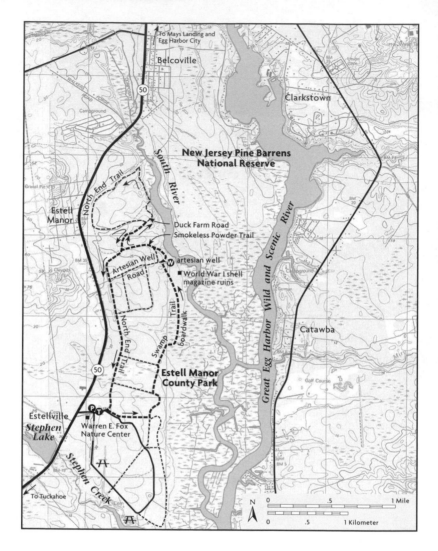

is surely enjoying trotting down this easy path, sniffing the scents. Detours lead to views of the South River, a branch of the Great Egg Harbor Wild and Scenic River System. At the end of the boardwalk, turn right and walk over to the pillarlike ruins of a shell magazine. Just in front of it, water pours from a suspended pipe. This artesian well, a great water source for you and your dog, reaches the Kirkwood Aquifer that extends south from Cherry Hill.

From the end of the boardwalk, go straight across Artesian Well Road onto the Smokeless Powder Trail. Remember, when no sign or blaze tells you to turn, stay on your course. The path goes through woods, edges a grassy parking lot, and passes around a gate. Keep your dog on a close leash. In some places, the trails are so infrequently used that their washboard surface feels like the railroad ties were just removed.

Turn right onto Duck Farm Road, part of the red-blazed North End Trail, and hike for 15 minutes to see the path, then turn around. Or, for an extra 2 miles, continue hiking on Duck Farm Road, which loops back. As you hike back on the North End Trail's sandy road, notice the trenches and mounds of soil above them. These trenches were dug in case it was necessary to protect the company. The trail leads back to the parking lot and nature center with natural and cultural history exhibits.

48. Historic Smithville Loop

Round-trip: 2.8 miles
Elevation range: 20–50 feet
Difficulty: Easy
Hiking time: 1.5 hours
Best canine hiking season: Late fall through June
Regulations: Dogs must be leashed
Maps: USGS Pemberton, NJ quadrangle; Burlington County Parks System, Historic Smithville Park
Information: Burlington County Parks System, (609) 265 5858, *www.co.burlington.nj.us/departments*

Getting there: From Interstate 295, take exit 47A (Mount Holly/Burlington) to County Route 541 South for a few miles and turn left at the light onto Woodlane Road (County Route 630). In 3 miles, turn right at another light onto Smithville Road (County Route 684). Go through the stop sign and make the second right into the park at the Park Avenue Access. Bear left onto North River Street and park by the water.

Take the blue Ravine Nature Trail up the steps, across the picnic area, and into the woods above Rancocas Creek, which flows west out of the Pine Barrens. The trail comes out on a road, briefly passing private property then turning right into a field before entering woods. It winds around and over a ravine on narrow wooden bridges. Farley, intimidated at first, soon became adept at this high-wire act. A few big sugar maple, red oak, and tulip trees dominate the woods.

Dr. Karen and Greta and friends frequently hike the trails of Historic Smithville. Here they enjoy the Yellow Trail.

Back to the parking lot, turn left and follow blue-blazed North River Street, an extension of the Ravine Nature Trail. Go past the old factories that, long ago, made textiles, woodworking machinery, and high-wheeled bicycles. Turn left onto the Red Trail and cross bridge D4.14, a metal truss bridge reminiscent of the historic factory bridge on the site.

Cross the parking lot and turn right onto the Green Trail toward the water. The sandy gravel path is pretty in winter, showing off the trees, and soft on your dog's feet. Several judiciously placed docks provide nice views over Smithville Lake and an experience for your canine pal. Soon, reach the Floating Trail, which goes over the lake. It sways and moves like a suspension bridge, a fun experience for you and your dog. Farley, unused to moving trails, first skulked with its movement, adding this to his increasing range of experiences. The Floating Trail won the 2005 Merit Award from the New Jersey Association of Landscape Architects and the 2005 Ruth Hughes Innovative Accessible Recreation Facility Award.

On land again, take the trail to the left into the woods and cross the wooden footbridge. At the top of the hill, bear right. Turn right onto the Yellow Trail, an abandoned railbed, then right into the woods on Green above the lake. This time, Farley was an old hand at bobbing over the Floating Trail.

For a longer hike through nice woods, take the Yellow Trail to the left as you leave the woods on Green. The Yellow Trail crosses the road and turns left. Turn right on the Red Trail, eventually hiking along Rancocas Creek back to your car.

Stop in at the park office in a historic house for information about the historic village. Use the side door. Smithville Village is listed on the national and New Jersey registers of historic places.

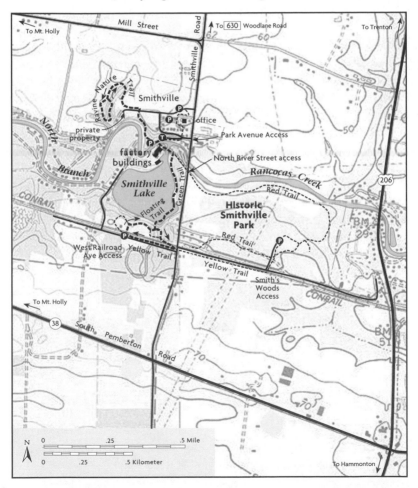

49. Parvin State Park Loop

Round-trip: 5.2 miles
Elevation range: 60–100 feet
Difficulty: Easy to lightly moderate
Hiking time: 2.5 hours
Best canine hiking season: Late fall through June
Regulations: Dogs must be on a 6-foot leash; dogs not allowed on
   beach
Maps: USGS Elmer, NJ quadrangle; NJDEP, Parvin State Park
Information: Parvin State Park, (856) 358-8616,
   www.njparksandforests.org

Getting there: Take Interstate 295 to exit 26 (State Route 42 South).
Go 0.1 mile and take State Route 55 South to exit 45 (County Route
553 South). At 6.8 miles, County Route 553 turns left at the light onto
Centerton Road. At 1.3 miles, turn left at the light onto Almond Road
(County Route 540 East). Drive 2.1 miles to the park office and lake on
the right. Park across the street on the left.

This hike gives you and your dog an up-close adventure through South
Jersey swamps, a lakeside ramble, equestrian paths in upland forest, and
an opportunity to see an abundance of small wildlife—notably reptiles
and migrating birds.

   With a map from the office (closed on winter weekends, but maps are
on an information board), head counterclockwise on the Parvin Lake

Wetland snake

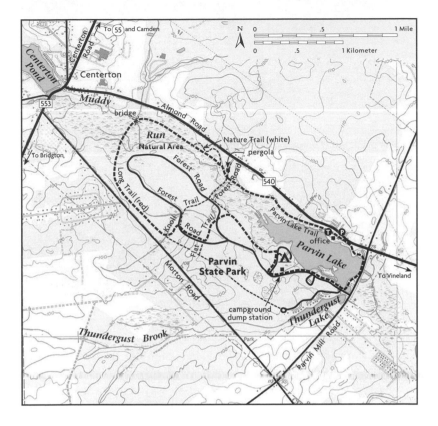

Trail, blazed green. The path descends through indigenous American holly trees, pines, sweet gum, southern red oak, and club moss, then eases through swampland where Atlantic white cedar and other trees and shrubs grow out of moss-covered mounds.

Here, the pitch pines grow tall and straight, unlike their gnarled and stunted representatives on the Kittatinny Ridge. The close-to-the-surface water table, which provides this watery habitat, enables their luxuriant growth.

At a junction, the green trail turns left, but go straight across the forest road through a pergola and onto the combined red Long Trail and white Nature Trail, unmarked here, into the Natural Area. Posts with blazes appear soon. Take a quick trip down to the Muddy Run, a Maurice River tributary, on the left. The white blazes leave to the right, but stay on the red Long Trail. The path gets very wet in spots as it travels across planks, stones, and fallen trees in the swamp. In early summer, your dog will keep cool on this trail as he enjoys the murky depths.

The Parvin Lake Trail blazes quickly through a variety of habitats, including this stretch of sunny woods.

Up on drier ground, hike through cedar, magnolia, holly, and bowers of black huckleberry shrubs that hug the path. If your pooch is tiny, you may have to carry him as you pick your best way across a few logs and plant hummocks. Perhaps he's used to being carried in a day pack?

Soon, cross an arched wooden bridge over the Muddy Run. At an unblazed Y intersection, go straight ahead through upland forest, still on the red-blazed trail. The woods become wide open and hikers won't see a blaze for a long while. Many unmarked paths cross the trail, but you cannot get lost, for roads border the park on all sides. All trails to the left join the blue-blazed Forest Road that ends at Parvin Mill Road, which intersects County Route 540 and the parking lot.

After a red blaze, turn left onto the orange-blazed Knoll Trail, hike 10 minutes and turn right onto the blue Forest Road for an easy walk, then turn left onto the pink Flat Trail. Go right on the green Parvin Lake Trail through open dry woods on a soft, sandy path, skirting the swamp.

At a trail crossroads, a campground-area sign announces "NO PETS." To avoid the campground, turn right and hike to the blue trail. Turn left onto Forest Road, then take the first path to the left after the campground dump station. The green trail flirts with the shore of Parvin Lake, sneaks through a fence back to the road, enters woods, passes over falls, crosses lawn and stream, and returns to the office. This is a fun hike through unusual habitats. You and your canine pal will enjoy it.

50. Sandy Hook: Beach and Dunes Loop

Round-trip: 5 miles
Elevation range: Flat
Difficulty: Moderate
Hiking time: 2.5 hours
Best canine hiking season: Day after Labor Day through March 14
Regulations: Dogs must be on a 6-foot leash
Maps: USGS Sandy Hook Overextended, NJ quadrangle
Information: Gateway National Recreation Area, Sandy Hook Unit,
    (732) 872-5970, *www.nps.gov/gate*

Getting there: From the Garden State Parkway take exit 117 to State Route 36 East for 12 miles. After crossing the bridge, turn right onto the

Black, leathery skate egg cases, or "mermaid's purse," are scattered on the beach. This one's four tendrils once hooked to seaweed.

island, following the signs to Sandy Hook. The visitor center is 2 miles farther on the right. Park in the next lot to stay a longer time.

Get ready for a workout! This sunny hike offers dog and human a fun time on the beach with sights and scents of the sea—a gentle surf, shells, soft paths, a lot of other dogs, and a hike through the largest American holly forest on the East Coast.

Nesting shorebirds, such as the federally endangered piping plover and least tern, and black skimmers, return to the area to nest on the beaches and dunes. Although ocean beaches are closed to dogs from March 15

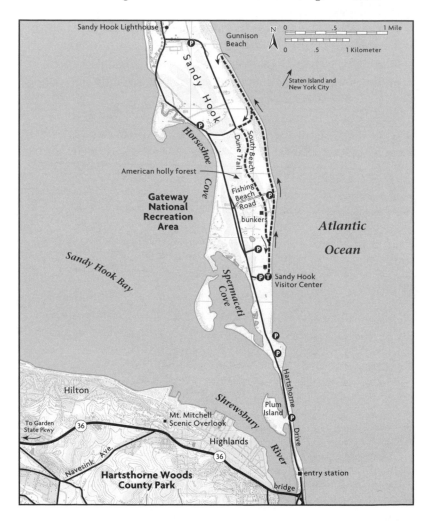

Dogs and their humans bond in nature. Pepe gives Lance an appreciative kiss on the beach at Sandy Hook.

through Labor Day, some birds may be nesting earlier. Stay on the trails. Bayside beaches are open year-round to dogs. For updated information on any beach closings or restrictions, ask at the visitor center when you arrive. It is open daily 10:00 AM to 5:00 PM.

From the visitor center, head to the beach! Turn left, heading north on the sand. A variety of shells still surface on this beach, as do skate egg cases and horseshoe crab shells. The shoreline, as it goes out to sea, undulates, and small pools of seawater may remain in the sand. In winter, these salty puddles might feel warm and good on Fido's feet. The range of activity on this beach will interest your dog: surf fishing, dog walking, and family get-togethers.

Pass a chimney of a defunct bunker sticking out of the dunes. Hike another hour to Gunnison Beach where the beach curves, revealing New York City across the ocean. In late afternoon, the sun reflects golden on the buildings of Staten Island.

Hike a bit more, then turn around and come back. Watch for a sign into the dunes that says "SOUTH BEACH DUNE TRAIL," and turn right onto the path. Notice the prickly pear, South Jersey's very own cactus. Notice the smooth, olive trunks of American holly and the chunky black bark of wild black cherry growing alongside. This maritime forest has a fairytale feel. Light blue bayberry bushes and wildflowers in fall give subtle beauty.

After 1.1 miles, the path jogs left at the road and, just past a bunker, into the dunes again. Soon it brings you out to the beach. Turn right into the parking lot. Carry water on this hike. If your dog has never been on a beach before, this is the place to take him.

After the hike, take your dog to see the oldest lighthouse in America, built in 1764 to guide ships into New York Harbor. The island's rich military history includes the protection of New York City during World War I and, later, the manufacture of NIKE air defense missiles.

51. Trenton-Hamilton Marsh

Round-trip: 4 miles
Elevation range: Flat
Difficulty: Easy
Hiking time: 2 hours
Best canine hiking season: Late fall through June
Regulations: Dogs must be leashed
Maps: USGS Trenton East, NJ quadrangle; New Jersey Trails
   Association
Information: Mercer County Park Commission, (609) 989-6559,
   www.mercercounty.org/parks; New Jersey Trails Association,
   www.njtrails.org

Getting there: From Interstate 295, take exit 61 (Arena Drive). Turn right at the second light onto Woodside Avenue. At 0.4 mile, turn right onto South Broad Street (US Highway 206 North). Turn left at the fifth light onto Sewell Avenue. Go four blocks to the end and turn left downhill to the John A. Roebling Park parking lot.

This section of John A. Roebling Park brings canine and human through the northernmost freshwater tidal marsh along the Delaware River. The extensive wetlands and associated woodlands attract migrating birds

Nearby residents, Earl and Heidi, hike daily on the Spring Lake Trail.

and their watchers. More than 875 vascular plant species; 237 bird, 23 amphibian and reptile, and 29 butterfly species; and at least 60 different kinds of fish live in its ponds, river and streams, uplands, swamp and marshes, floodplain and bluffs. Your dog will love the cool feel of moist soil, the flurry of winged activity, and the sociability of a popular spot among the local dogs and their human pals. Springtime brings a lot of wildflowers and fragrant magnolias for two-legged hikers to enjoy, unless your dog loves sniffing flowers, too.

Take the Spring Lake Trail to the right of Spring Lake that sidles between lake and marsh. Slip down to the marsh and peek through phragmites at ducks, geese, and swans on the water. Cross the bridge into deciduous woods and bear right, following the yellow blazes, which

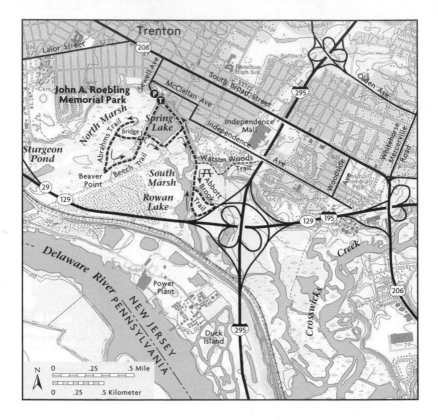

circle the island; the trail has different names on each side of the island. Take the first right spur to the edge of the North Marsh, a birder's heaven, adorned with bird and duck boxes. Look for a beaver dam to the right.

Continue on yellow, now called the Abrahms Trail, along the marsh to Beaver Point where it becomes the Beech Trail along the South Marsh. Swans are everywhere. Your dog will be entertained. After crossing a stream, the yellow trail brings you to the bridge again, but if you end up on the aqua trail instead, just keep bearing right.

Cross the bridge and turn right, hiking around the lake. Turn right on the dirt road between the mudflats of Rowan Lake and a hillside with large beech trees whose roots look like giant hands grasping the soil. At the end, go around the gate and turn right onto the dirt road.

Turn into the picnic area on the left about midway and take the yellow-blazed Abbott Brook Trail back. This trail may be inundated after heavy rain or during high tide. If so, just turn around and head back on the dirt road.

For a longer hike after coming to the dirt crossroads, turn right into the woods on the red-blazed Watson Woods Trail that climbs 40 feet to a bluff.

A lot of sights and scents abound to give your dog a fun hike.

52. Wells Mills Loop

Round-trip: 6.7 miles
Elevation range: 50–130 feet
Difficulty: Moderate
Hiking time: 3.5 hours
Best canine hiking season: Late fall through June
Regulations: Dogs must be leashed; no smoking
Maps: USGS Brookville, NJ quadrangle; Ocean County Parks and
   Recreation, Wells Mills County Park
Information: Wells Mills County Park, (609) 971-3085,
   www.oceancountyparks.org

Getting there: From the Garden State Parkway, take exit 74 (Forked River) and turn right onto Lacey Road. Turn right onto US Highway 9 South at 2.4 miles and right onto County Route 532 at 3.4 miles. The park entrance is 4.4 miles on the left. A word of caution: At the last toll booth on the Garden State Parkway, coming and leaving, be sure to have exact change of 25 cents (as of 2006) handy because the booth is not staffed.

This 900-acre park in the Pine Barrens has a lot to offer canine and human hikers—short, steep hills, one of the prettiest cedar swamps, a lake with geese and ducks, and creek crossings.

At the kiosk near the parking lot, sign the trail log that lets someone know you are there. From the nature center, head toward Wells Mills Lake and turn right onto the white-blazed Penns Hill Trail that encircles the park. Fido will enjoy the gaggle of white geese that may squawk by.

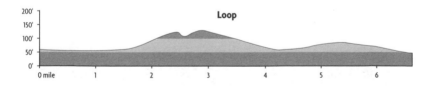

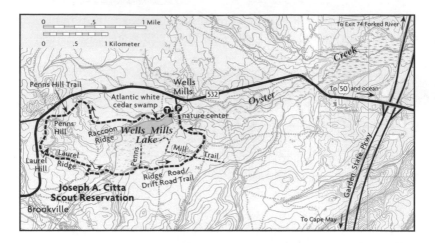

Only eight geese remain of the original thirty that the park inherited fifteen years ago.

Enter a wonderful Atlantic white cedar swamp where the soft footpath weaves among trees over moss-covered roots. The verdant moss-tinted boles of cedar, American holly, pitch pine, and mountain laurel make the route look like a maze through a garden.

The path crosses a sand road, one of many, and rambles along a hillside covered in pitch pine, blueberry, and huckleberry. Hike 1 mile to Raccoon Ridge, the first of three sand hills more than a hundred feet high. The trail crosses seeps on skinny footbridges as it meanders up and around Penns Hill at 2.4 miles and Laurel Hill at 2.9 miles. Stop on a hilltop with a perfectly placed bench for a water break.

The trail goes along Laurel Ridge, passing expectedly through long, dense thickets of mountain laurel. At a log fence, the trail turns right, joining the yellow- and green-blazed trails. At this point, the trail enters the Joseph A. Citta Scout Reservation, private property, for about 0.75 mile. Soon, the path turns left into the forest. Cross Oyster Creek, which feeds the human-made lake, at 4.1 miles, then pass through stands of oak and berry, cedar and laurel.

The white trail turns left, but you follow the multiuse yellow-blazed Ridge Road/Drift Road Trail. Descending gently, reach Oyster Creek Bridge with close-up views of young, fluffy, Atlantic white cedar trees.

Opposite: Resident geese on Wells Mills Lake provide great interest to Farley.

Take a brief walk out on the dam to admire the glassine lake of dark water surrounded by dark trees with white geese.

Deer browse comfortably in the meadow surrounding the nature center, so keep a tight leash on your dog when crossing here. Sign out in the trail log. Bring plenty of water.

APPENDIX A

Off-Leash Dog Parks

Bergen County: (201) 336-7275, *www.co.bergen.nj.us/parks*
Riverside County Park—North Area, Riverside Avenue, Lyndhurst
Overpeck County Park—South Area, Fort Lee Road, Leonia
Wood Dale County Park, Prospect Avenue, Woodcliff Lake
Hours: 10:00 AM to sunset
Camden County Parks: (856) 795-7275,
www.co.camden.nj.us/government/offices
Pooch Park at Cooper River Park, North Park Drive, Cherry Hill
Hours: 6:00 AM to 10:00 PM
Denville Township Health Department: (973) 625-8300, ext. 265,
www.denvillenj.org/happy_hound_playground_at_cooks.htm
Cooks Pond, 455 Diamond Spring Road, Denville
Hours: 8:00 AM to dusk, Thursday, Saturday, Sunday, Monday, fee
Essex County Department of Parks: (973) 228-8776,
www.last-exit.net/essexcounty
Watsessing Park, Bloomfield Avenue and Conger Streets, Bloomfield
Hours: Daybreak to 10:00 PM
Hudson County Park System: (201) 915-1386,
www.hudsoncountynj.org
Stephen R. Gregg Bayonne Park, 46th Street, Bayonne
James J. Braddock North Hudson Park, 81st Street, North Bergen
Hours: Sunrise to sunset
Hunterdon County Department of Parks and Recreation:
(908) 782-1158, *www.co.hunterdon.nj.us*
Off-leash area on the grounds of County Complex, State Route 12,
   Raritan Township
Hours: Sunrise to sunset
Mercer County Park Commission: (609) 989-6533,
www.mercercounty.org
Mercer County Park, 334 South Post Road, Princeton Junction
Hours: Sunrise to sunset
Middlesex County Parks and Recreation: (732) 745-4593,
www.co.middlesex.nj.us
Thompson Park, Perrineville Road and Forsgate Drive, Jamesburg
Donaldson Park, Second Avenue, Highland Park
Hours: Dawn to dusk

Monmouth County Park System: 732-842-4000,
www.monmouthcountyparks.com
Thompson Park, 805 Newman Springs Road (County Route 520),
Lincroft
Hours: 8:00 AM to dusk

Morris County Park Commission: (973) 326-7600,
www.morrisparks.net
Lewis Morris County Park–Old Army Area, Mendham Road, Morris
Township
Hours: 9:00 AM to sunset

Ocean County Department of Parks and Recreation: (732) 341-3243, *www.co.ocean.nj.us*
Robert J. Miller Air Park, County Route 530, Berkeley Township
Ocean County Park, State Route 88, Lakewood Township
Hours: 8:00 AM to 8:00 PM, annual fee and permit

Passaic County Parks Department: (973) 881-4832,
www.passaiccountynj.org
Goffle Brook Park, Goffle Road, Hawthorne
Hours: Sunrise to sunset

Salem County Parks: (856) 935-7510 ext. 8604, *www.salemcounty.org*
Camp Crockett, 148 Avis Mill Road, Piles Grove
Hours: 8:30 AM to 4:00 PM

Somerset County Park Commission: (732) 873-2695,
www.somersetcountyparks.org
Colonial Park, Mettlers Road, Somerset
Hours: Dawn to dusk

Union County: (908) 527-4900, *www.unioncountynj.org*
Echo Lake Park, two entrances—Springfield Avenue, Westfield and
Mountain Avenue and State Route 22, Mountainside
Hours: Dawn to dusk

APPENDIX B

Wildlife Management Areas and Dog-Training Areas

The public can exercise or train dogs off leash on 299,000 acres in any of 119 statewide Wildlife Management Areas (WMA) from September 1 to April 30, except for the Friday before opening day of the regular small game season. Additionally, anyone may exercise or train a dog in any Dog Training Area—designated areas within certain WMAs—year-round, except for the Friday before opening day of the regular small game season. Check the website for hunting season dates.

Off-leash Dog Training Areas are open to the public and have been used historically for training hunting dogs. Be courteous. Your dog is not permitted to "run at large," meaning that, although he is off leash, you must have him under control at all times.

Maps: *www.state.nj.us/dep/fgw/wmaland.htm*

Regulations: Dogs must be licensed and under control.

Information: NJDEP, Division of Fish and Wildlife, Bureau of Land Management, (609) 984-0547, *www.fishandwildlife.com*, annual hunting issue of the *Fish and Wildlife Digest*

The following eleven WMAs contain Dog Training Areas:

1. Assunpink East, Monmouth County
2. Black River, Morris County
3. Clinton East, Hunterdon County
4. Colliers Mills South, Ocean County
5. Glassboro, Gloucester County
6. Hainesville, Sussex County
7. Manasquan River, Ocean County
8. Millville, Cumberland County
9. Stafford Forge South, Ocean County
10. Tuckahoe North, Atlantic and Cape May Counties
11. Whittingham, Fredon Township, Sussex County

APPENDIX C

Resources

Dog Packs and Trail Supplies
www.wolfpacks.com
www.epetpals.com
www.arcatapet.com
www.sitstay.com
www.youractivepet.com
www.jandd.com
www.reshaequip.com
www.rei.com

Websites About Hiking with Dogs
www.hikewithyourdog.com
www.catskillhikes.com
www.k9trailblazers.org/dog_hiking_resource.htm
www.njdoghikes.com

BIBLIOGRAPHY

Acker, Randy, and Jim Fergus. *Field Guide: Dog First Aid Emergency Care for the Hunting, Working, and Outdoor Dog (Field Guide).* Wilderness Adventures Press, 1994.

Collins, Beryl Robichaud, and Karl H. Anderson. *Plant Communities of New Jersey.* Rutgers University Press, 1994.

Fogle, Bruce, and Amanda Williams. *First Aid for Dogs: What to Do when Emergencies Happen,* (reprint edition), Penguin Books, 1997.

Hoffman, Gary. *Dogs on the Trail.* InsightOut Publishing, 2005.

LaBelle, Charlene. *Backpacking with Your Dog.* Alpine Publications, 2004.

New York–New Jersey Trail Conference. *New Jersey Walk Book,* 2nd ed. New York–New Jersey Trail Conference, 2004

Scherer, Glenn. *Nature Walks in New Jersey.* Appalachian Mountain Club Books, 1998

Scofield, Bruce, Stella Green, and H. Neil Zimmerman. *50 Hikes in New Jersey,* 2nd ed. Backcountry Publications, 1997.

INDEX

ABOUT THE AUTHOR AND THE DOGS

Mary Jasch is publisher/editor of *DIG IT! Magazine*, covering East Coast gardens tame and wild. Mary's love for the woods and writing is enhanced by a late-in-life degree in natural resources management from Rutgers, The State University of New Jersey. Her freelance articles and photographs about nature and hiking with dogs appear in regional magazines and newspapers. Mary has four dogs, all littermates—Farley, Little One, Petey, and Tank, born in 1995 from German shepherd mama Arnuk and pound-dog father Broadway. Mary and gang did a brief two-year stint as a recreational sled dog team. Beasts and the beauty then took to the woods at a human's pace, hiking the trails of New Jersey and beyond.

To learn more about the author and her dogs, and hiking New Jersey, visit *www.njdoghikes.com*.

THE MOUNTAINEERS, founded in 1906, is a nonprofit outdoor activity and conservation club, whose mission is "to explore, study, preserve, and enjoy the natural beauty of the outdoors...." Based in Seattle, Washington, the club is now the third-largest such organization in the United States, with seven branches throughout Washington State.

The Mountaineers sponsors both classes and year-round outdoor activities in the Pacific Northwest, which include hiking, mountain climbing, ski-touring, snowshoeing, bicycling, camping, kayaking, nature study, sailing, and adventure travel. The club's conservation division supports environmental causes through educational activities, sponsoring legislation, and presenting informational programs.

All club activities are led by skilled, experienced instructors, who are dedicated to promoting safe and responsible enjoyment and preservation of the outdoors.

If you would like to participate in these organized outdoor activities or the club's programs, consider a membership in The Mountaineers. For information and an application, write or call The Mountaineers, Club Headquarters, 300 Third Avenue West, Seattle, WA 98119; 206-284-6310. You can also visit the club's website at www.mountaineers.org or contact The Mountaineers via email at clubmail@mountaineers.org.

The Mountaineers Books, an active, nonprofit publishing program of the club, produces guidebooks, instructional texts, historical works, natural history guides, and works on environmental conservation. All books produced by The Mountaineers Books fulfill the club's mission.

Send or call for our catalog of more than 500 outdoor titles:

The Mountaineers Books
1001 SW Klickitat Way, Suite 201
Seattle, WA 98134
800-553-4453
mbooks@mountaineersbooks.org
www.mountaineersbooks.org

The Mountaineers Books is proud to be a corporate sponsor of The Leave No Trace Center for Outdoor Ethics, whose mission is to promote and inspire responsible outdoor recreation through education, research, and partnerships. The Leave No Trace program is focused specifically on human-powered (nonmotorized) recreation.

Leave No Trace strives to educate visitors about the nature of their recreational impacts, as well as offer techniques to prevent and minimize such impacts. Leave No Trace is best understood as an educational and ethical program, not as a set of rules and regulations.

For more information, visit www.LNT.org, or call 800-332-4100.

OTHER TITLES YOU MIGHT ENJOY FROM THE MOUNTAINEERS BOOKS

Best Hikes with Dogs: New York City and Beyond, *Tammy L. McCarley*
City and surrounding area hikes both you and your dog will love.

Best Hikes with Children in New Jersey, 2nd Edition, *Arlene Zatz*
Great walks for little ones, with tips for keeping kids interested in the outdoors.

Tent and Car Camper's Handbook: Advice for Families & First-Timers, *Buck Tilton*
The lowdown on family car and tent camping—no experience necessary!

Day Hiker's Handbook: Get Started with the Experts, *Mike Lanza*
A stronger body and refreshed spirit begin with a single step. Start today.

**Outdoors Online
An Internet Guide to Everything Wild & Green,** *Erika Dillman*
Everything you wanted to know about the outdoors but couldn't find on the Web.

Digital Photography Outdoors: A Field Guide for Travel & Adventure Photographers
James Martin
The secrets to shooting great outdoor images with your digital camera.

**Conditioning for Outdoor Fitness:
A Comprehensive Training Guide,** 2nd Edition, *David Musnick, M.D. and Mark Pierce, A.T.C.*
Pick a sport; find the exercises that will get you fit to participate.

Mountaineers Books has more than 500 outdoor recreation titles in print.
Receive a free catalog at
www.mountaineersbooks.org.